THE LEFTOVERS COOKBOOK

Abridged Edition

by LOYTA WOODING

GROSSET & DUNLAP
A NATIONAL GENERAL COMPANY

Publishers   *New York*

For Ralph and Laurel
Ray and Judy

GROSSET & DUNLAP SPECIAL ABRIDGED EDITION 1972
BY ARRANGEMENT WITH DAVID WHITE, INC., PUBLISHERS

PRINTED IN THE UNITED STATES OF AMERICA

CONTENTS

FOREWORD

By definition, a good cook is a person who respects food. Consequently, the problem of what to do with leftovers has plagued cooks since cooking began. To throw away good food offends not only the sense of financial thrift but the feeling that something potentially delicious is not being used.

Naturally the problem is less serious in a large family, whose members are given to raiding the refrigerator for after school or bedtime snacks. I myself became increasingly aware of it as my own family diminished from a full house to two people and finally to only one. Old habits were so strong that for some time I continued to plan meals as I had previously done, unwilling to give up baked hams, succulent turkeys, juicy roasts, and other delights of large-scale cooking. As a result my refrigerator was constantly crowded with leftovers, many of which were eventually doomed to become garbage. Finding myself appalled by the waste of that aromatic stuffing, that cup of rice, those slices of fried eggplant, that half-bowl of waffle batter, I came to realize that with imagination and ingenuity I could use any and all leftovers in the concoction of new and delicious dishes.

My success has been proved by the number of times that I have had to confess to enthusiastic guests that the meal they were praising had been partly based on a leftover this or that. I began to be besieged with requests for suggestions on what could be done with "all that gravy, it's a shame to throw away" or that cup of "perfectly good mashed potatoes."

The next step, logically enough, was to start a file on these suggestions, and from that file, which rapidly assumed large proportions, came the genesis of this book.

Another logical development was the idea of planning several meals at the same time, all based on one large cut of meat as the basis of two or three main dishes with varied accompaniments, thus converting leftovers into "planned-overs." This system avoids the boring results of simply reheating and re-serving, which is really what gives leftovers their bad name. Instead, the recipes here defy any connoisseur to identify the leftover ingredients used.

The aim of the book is to provide menus which use food—for the first, second, or even third time—to create imaginative and nutritionally balanced meals. The unusual dishes in these menus are marked by an asterik to indicate that the recipe is included; these recipes either follow the particular menu or can be found by consulting the index. Dishes not so marked are suggestions for accompaniments, for which recipes can be found in any basic cookbook. The cook who gets into the spirit of this novel method will soon begin developing variations, often based on different leftovers that turn up in her—or his—own refrigerator. In short, what I hope to provide here is not so much a cookbook as a technique.

Loyta Wooding

THE PLANNED-OVERS

Even the most inexperienced food-shopper quickly learns that large cuts of meat are much less expensive per serving than the smaller cuts. What is less obvious but equally important is that by planning ahead to make several meals from the same large cut, much of the preparation can be done for the first meal, thus saving time and effort as well as money. Here your freezer or freezing compartment is invaluable, since meal-sized portions can be stored, and only the amount needed for each meal thawed.

For example, if you buy 6 or 7 pounds of economical chuck (a pot roast with a round bone, which has fine flavor and little waste), you can have delicious New England Beef the first day, a juicy meat pie a day or two later, and a hearty and nourishing soup for yet another day.

BEEF

CHUCK ROAST—ONE

Buy a 6- to 7-pound chuck roast of beef and plan three distinct meals, four servings each.

MEAL NO. 1

New England Beef with
Massachusetts Horseradish Sauce

Boiled Potatoes
Sautéed Cabbage   Mixed Green Salad
Baked Apples

1

MEAL NO. 2

Savoy House Beef Pie

Browned Parsnips   Cheese-stuffed Celery
Lettuce Wedges   Russian Dressing
Peach Melba

MEAL NO. 3

Old-Fashioned Hearty Soup

French Bread with Welsh Rarebit
Crisp Relishes
Sherbet   Cookies

New England Beef

6 to 7 pounds chuck roast
1 onion, halved
2 carrots, sliced
1 stalk celery, sliced
4 sprigs of parsley

1 green onion, sliced
1 bay leaf
1½ tablespoons salt
1 teaspoon peppercorns
Massachusetts Horseradish Sauce

Place meat in a large, heavy kettle; add onion, carrots, celery, parsley, green onion, bay leaf, salt, and peppercorns. Add enough water just to cover meat; cover and bring to a boil. Reduce heat; simmer 2½ to 3 hours or until meat is fork tender. Remove meat to a heated platter; keep warm while making sauce. Strain broth; skim off fat. Measure 2 cups broth for sauce; refrigerate remainder for soup. Slice beef; serve with Massachusetts Horseradish Sauce. Makes 4 servings with meat left over.

Massachusetts Horseradish Sauce

3 tablespoons butter or margarine
⅓ cup flour
2 cups skimmed broth
½ teaspoon instant minced onion

¼ cup prepared horseradish
½ teaspoon salt
dash Worcestershire sauce

Melt butter in a small saucepan; stir in flour and blend well. Heat slowly, stirring constantly, until flour is browned. Remove from heat; stir in broth and onion. Cook for 1 minute, stirring constantly until sauce thickens and boils. Measure out 1 cup of sauce; refrigerate and reserve for Savoy House Beef Pie. Stir horseradish into remaining 1 cup. Season with salt and Worcestershire sauce. Serve hot. Makes about 1¼ cups.

Savoy House Beef Pie

3 cups cubed cooked beef	dash of Tabasco
1 small onion	1 package (2 envelopes) instant
1 cup reserved brown sauce (See	mashed potatoes
Mass. Horseradish Sauce)	2 tablespoons chopped parsley
½ teaspoon Worcestershire sauce	1 tablespoon minced celery

Heat oven to 350°F. Coarsely chop beef pieces and onion; stir into brown sauce. Add Worcestershire sauce and Tabasco; heat in large saucepan to boiling. Prepare instant mashed potatoes according to package directions; stir in parsley and celery. Spread half the potato mixture in a buttered, shallow 1½-quart baking dish; spoon hot meat mixture over. Top with remaining potatoes, swirling them in a circle. Bake 25 to 30 minutes or until pie is heated through and potatoes are lightly browned. Makes 4 servings.

Old-Fashioned Hearty Soup

6 cups skimmed, chilled broth	1 small turnip, chopped
¾ cup finely diced carrots	¾ teaspoon salt
¾ cup finely diced celery	⅛ teaspoon pepper
¾ cup finely diced onions	

Combine broth and vegetables in a large saucepan; simmer 15 minutes or until vegetables are crisply tender. Season with salt and pepper. Serve hot. Makes 4 servings.

CHUCK ROAST—TWO

Have the butcher cut off about 2½ pounds from a 5- to 6-pound beef chuck roast, leaving the remaining piece intact. Then plan the following three meals.

MEAL NO. 1

Austrian Pot Roast

Mushroom Soufflé   Buttered Broccoli
French Fried Onion Rings
Orange Sherbet with Bourbon

MEAL NO. 2

Beef Salad Japonais

Hash Browned Potato Patties
Canned Tomato Aspic
Chocolate Angel Cake

MEAL NO. 3

Greek Beef with Chestnuts

Spinach with Pine Nuts
Anchovy Salad
Fresh Berry Tarts

Austrian Pot Roast

The Austrians are very proud of their coffee and they often include it in cooking for a piquant flavor.

3 to 3½ pounds chuck roast of beef
¼ teaspoon cumin
1 teaspoon black pepper
½ teaspoon Tabasco
2 tablespoons flour

2 tablespoons beef fat or shortening
1 cup consommé
¼ cup cold coffee
2 medium onions, sliced
1 teaspoon salt
¼ teaspoon pepper

Rub beef with mixture of cumin, black pepper, and Tabasco. Dust with flour. Melt beef fat in a Dutch oven; add meat and brown on all sides. Add remaining ingredients; cover and simmer 2 to 2½ hours, or until meat is tender. Makes 4 servings.

Beef Salad Japonais

A quick gourmet dish with an Oriental touch.

2 cups cooked Austrian pot roast, diced
½ cup water chestnuts, sliced
½ cup mayonnaise
1 teaspoon Dijon-type mustard

1 dill pickle, finely chopped
¾ cup chopped celery hearts
crisp lettuce leaves
2 hard-cooked eggs, sliced
few sprigs parsley

Combine meat with chestnuts, mayonnaise, mustard, pickle, and celery hearts. Pile lightly onto lettuce leaves. Garnish with egg slices and parsley. Makes 4 servings.

Greek Beef with Chestnuts

I have been served this dish in several restaurants in the lovely Peloponnesus area of Greece.

2½ pounds beef chuck, cut into
  2-inch cubes
¾ teaspoon salt
⅛ teaspoon pepper
water
2 pounds chestnuts

1 medium onion, minced
1 cup hot consommé
1 tablespoon sugar
4 slices bread
2 tablespoons butter

Place meat in a heavy skillet; sprinkle with salt and pepper. Add water to cover. Cover skillet tightly; cook over medium heat 1 to 1½ hours, or until meat is tender. While meat is cooking, prepare chestnuts as follows. Heat oven to 400°F. Slash shells of chestnuts; place in a baking pan, and bake 15 minutes. Cool, then peel off shells and skins, being careful not to break the chestnuts. Set aside.

Remove meat and liquid from skillet and reserve. Skim 2 tablespoons fat from reserved liquid and return to skillet. Add onion and sauté until limp. Add meat and chestnuts. Add consommé and remaining liquid. In a small pan caramelize the sugar with 1 teaspoon hot water. When it is a rich brown color, add to meat. Cover and cook 35 minutes. To make croutons, cut bread into cubes, discarding crusts; brown in butter. Turn meat onto a platter and surround with chestnuts and croutons. Makes 4 servings.

TOP ROUND STEAK—ONE

A 4- to 5-pound top round of beef can yield a substantial Sunday dinner and two delicious leftover meals for the family.

MEAL NO. 1

Beefsteak Parisienne

Green Beans Amandine
Corn Soufflé
Cucumber Salad Bowl
Orange Ring Cake

MEAL NO. 2

Stroganoff Burgers

French Fried Potatoes
Lettuce Wedges   Herb Mayonnaise
Celery Stalks
Jellied Fruit
Cookies

MEAL NO. 3

Beef Astoria

Stewed Tomatoes   Green Beans
Bibb Lettuce Salad
Plantation Pie

Beefsteak Parisienne

One of the many adopted American dishes served in Parisian restaurants.

4 to 5 pounds top round of beef
½ teaspoon pepper
½ teaspoon oregano
¾ teaspoon salt
2 tablespoons olive oil
1 clove garlic, minced
2 large green peppers, thinly sliced
1 red pepper, thinly sliced

¼ cup butter
1½ cups chopped celery
3 sprigs parsley
½ cup large stuffed green olives, halved
2 tablespoons capers
3 cups whole canned tomatoes, drained

Heat oven to 400°F. Lightly score the meat and rub in mixture of pepper, oregano, and salt. Pour olive oil into a shallow roasting pan. Add minced garlic and meat. Roast 35 minutes. Reduce heat to 350°F. and roast 1½ hours or until meat is tender. Sauté the green and red peppers in the butter; stir in the celery, parsley, and olives. Add sautéed mixture to roast with the capers and tomatoes; continue roasting 25 minutes. Serve meat on a heated platter with the vegetable sauce poured over it. Makes 6 servings.

Stroganoff Burgers

Here is an interesting variation of this ever-popular dish.

4 slices bacon, diced
½ cup chopped onion
1½ tablespoons flour
¼ teaspoon paprika
¾ teaspoon salt
⅛ teaspoon pepper

1 can (10½ ounces) condensed cream of mushroom soup
1½ cups cooked roast beef, ground
1 cup commercial sour cream
1 tablespoon chopped parsley
4 hamburger buns, split

Sauté bacon and onion in a medium skillet over moderate heat until lightly browned. Blend in flour, paprika, salt, and pepper. Stir in mushroom soup; add meat. Cook over low heat, stirring frequently until thickened. Fold in sour cream and parsley; heat, stirring gently. Spoon mixture over buns. Makes 4 servings.

Beef Astoria

4 tablespoons butter
3 medium potatoes, pared, finely diced
½ teaspoon salt
⅛ teaspoon pepper
1 small onion, chopped
1 tablespoon chopped green pepper
2 tablespoons tomato sauce

¾ cup leftover gravy
3 tablespoons dry red wine
1 tablespoon chopped parsley
⅛ teaspoon basil
2 cups coarsely chopped cooked beef
½ teaspoon paprika

Heat 3 tablespoons of the butter in a large, heavy skillet; add the potatoes and sauté, stirring frequently, until well browned. Season with salt and pepper. In another skillet melt remaining tablespoon of butter; add onion and green pepper and sauté lightly. Stir in tomato sauce, gravy, wine, parsley, basil, and beef. Bring mixture to a boil. Stir in half the browned potatoes. Turn onto a heated serving platter. Top with remaining potatoes; sprinkle with paprika and serve. Makes 4 servings.

TOP ROUND STEAK—TWO

Have your butcher divide a 4½-pound piece of top round steak as follows: Cut 1½ pounds into ½-inch cubes. Grind up 1 pound. Reserve the remaining 2-pound piece for Beefsteak in Foil.

MEAL NO. 1

Donon Beefsteak and Kidney Pie

Potatoes au Gratin
Crisp Green Salad with
Bacon Bits
Blueberry Pudding

MEAL NO. 2

Baked Stuffed Eggplant Isis

Garlic Whipped Potatoes
Buttered Carrots
Tomato and Cucumber Salad
Apple Turnovers

MEAL NO. 3

Beefsteak in Foil

Buttered Lima Beans
Glazed Beets in Orange Sauce
Tossed Salad
Almond Torte

Donon Beefsteak and Kidney Pie

1½ pounds beef kidneys	1½ cups canned whole baby carrots
1½ pounds round steak, cut in	⅛ teaspoon thyme
½-inch cubes	⅛ teaspoon basil
¼ cup flour	¼ cup sherry
½ teaspoon salt	2 tablespoons flour
½ cup shortening	1 tablespoon Worcestershire sauce
1½ cups boiling water	dash Tabasco
1 thin slice lemon	⅛ teaspoon dry mustard
1½ cups canned small white onions	1 package pie crust mix

Wash kidneys; split, remove fat and large tubes. Soak in salted water 1 hour.
Drain kidneys. Cut crosswise into ½-inch slices. Roll meats in flour mixed
with salt; brown in shortening in a heavy skillet. Remove to a heavy sauce-

pan; add boiling water and lemon. Simmer 1 hour. Add onions, carrots, and spices. Combine sherry with flour, Worcestershire sauce, Tabasco, and mustard; blend well. Add to mixture. Stir and cook until thickened. Heat oven to 425°F. Divide mixture among 4 large individual heatproof casseroles. Prepare pie crust mix according to package directions. Roll out to ⅛ inch thickness. Cut into 4 portions and cover casseroles. Flute edges, prick tops, and bake casseroles 25 minutes. Makes 4 servings.

Baked Stuffed Eggplant Isis

As a child I was introduced to this delicate dish in Egypt, and it became one of my family's and my own favorites.

4 small eggplants (about 5 inches long)
2 tablespoons vegetable oil
1 onion, chopped
1 pound ground round steak
½ cup dry wine
1½ teaspoons salt
⅛ teaspoon pepper
⅛ teaspoon paprika
1 teaspoon chopped parsley
¼ teaspoon sage
½ cup water
1 egg
½ cup grated Parmesan cheese
¼ cup light cream
¼ cup milk
¼ teaspoon onion salt

Cut eggplants in half lengthwise; scoop out centers and reserve for filling. Place eggplant shells in heavily salted water; let stand 30 minutes. Rinse in cold water; dry with absorbent paper. Heat oil in a medium skillet. Add onion and meat; brown well. Chop eggplant centers and add to mixture. Add the wine, salt, pepper, and paprika. Add parsley and sage and stir until well blended. Heat oven to 350°F. Stuff eggplant shells with mixture; place in shallow baking pan. Pour water around, and bake 40 minutes. Beat egg lightly and add remaining ingredients; pour mixture over stuffed eggplant and brown under broiler. Makes 4 servings.

Beefsteak in Foil

2 pounds round steak, cut into 4 equal-sized pieces
1½ teaspoons salt
½ teaspoon pepper
½ teaspoon celery salt
3 tablespoons lemon juice
4 tablespoons butter
2 large onions, chopped
4 green onions, chopped
1 cup canned tomatoes
4 tablespoons dry wine
½ teaspoon dill seed
2 tablespoons olive oil
4 slices processed American cheese

Rub meat with ½ the salt, the pepper and celery salt. Place in a shallow baking dish, add lemon juice and let stand 1 hour, turning frequently. Melt butter in a skillet; add onions and green onions and sauté until lightly browned. Add tomatoes, wine, and dill seed. Cover; simmer 15 minutes or until sauce is thick. Remove from heat; cool. In another skillet, brown meat on both sides in olive oil. Cut 4 12-inch squares of aluminum foil. Place 1 portion of meat in the center of each square and divide sauce equally over each. Place 1 slice of cheese on each. Fold securely and seal. Place on baking sheet. Bake 2 hours at 325°F. Makes 4 servings.

BEEF TENDERLOIN

The beef tenderloin is the aristocrat of meats. For company plan to serve Tenderloin Kobe Style. Order a 10-pound piece, cut off 1 three-pound and 1 one-pound piece for subsequent meals.

MEAL NO. 1

Tenderloin Kobe Style

Buttered Peas   Wild Rice
Bean Sprout and Pimiento Salad
Nesselrode Pie

MEAL NO. 2

Fillet of Beef Chateâu

Fluffy Rice   Stewed Tomatoes
Tossed Salad
Cherry Pie

MEAL NO. 3

Beef Tenderloin Josephine

Shoestring Potatoes   Glazed Carrots
Avocado on Bibb Lettuce
with French Dressing
Peach Melba

Tenderloin Kobe Style

Japan is famous for its Kobe beef. The chef of the Okura Hotel gave me this recipe on a recent visit to Tokyo.

6 pounds beef tenderloin
2 tablespoons olive oil
1 tablespoon coarse salt
1 teaspoon thyme

½ teaspoon sage
2 cloves garlic, unpeeled
½ cup dry white wine

Heat oven to 375°F. Rub meat with olive oil. Sprinkle with salt and herbs. Place meat in a shallow baking pan and add garlic. Bake 35 minutes. Meat will be rare. Remove garlic and discard. Pour wine into pan; heat thoroughly and serve with meat. Makes 8 servings.

Fillet of Beef Château

3 pounds beef tenderloin
½ cup olive oil
1 teaspoon pickling spices
1 large bay leaf

½ cup Madeira
1 onion, sliced
16 large mushrooms

Remove fat from beef; cut beef into 1½-inch cubes. Combine oil, pickling spices, bay leaf, wine, and onion slices separated in rings. Place meat in a shallow dish; pour marinade over it. Refrigerate overnight. To prepare fillet, remove stems from mushrooms, parboil mushrooms in lightly salted water 2 minutes, then drain and dry. Skewer meat and mushrooms alternately on 8-inch skewers. Broil 3 to 4 inches from source of heat 7 to 10 minutes, depending upon desired doneness. Serve immediately. Makes 6 servings.

Beef Tenderloin Josephine

1 pound beef tenderloin, sliced
  paper-thin
½ cup dry red wine
¼ cup tarragon vinegar
¼ cup lemon juice
1 tablespoon minced onion

1 teaspoon salt
⅛ teaspoon pepper
1 jar (2 ounces) red caviar
1 tablespoon minced chives
½ cup commercial sour cream
1 teaspoon finely chopped fresh dill

Place meat slices in a broiler-proof glass casserole. Combine wine, vinegar, and lemon juice, pour over meat, and toss lightly. Sprinkle with onion, salt and pepper. Refrigerate 3 hours. When ready to serve, drain meat and flatten slices with a spatula. Broil 3 inches from source of heat 1 minute on each side. Place all meat slices on a large, heated platter. Divide caviar among the slices, placing a dollop in each center. Sprinkle with chives, top with sour cream, sprinkle with dill. Serve immediately. Makes 4 servings.

RUMP ROAST

Buy a 6-pound rump roast of beef and cook it according to the following recipe, Sauerbraten American Style. Now, you may get either one or two additional meals from the leftovers, depending on your appetite and the size of your family. I suggest that you read the second two recipes, note the amounts of leftover Sauerbraten called for in each—and then make your decision.

MEAL NO. 1

**Sauerbraten American Style
with Noodles**

Silvered Carrots and Celery
Shredded Lettuce Salad
Apple Pie

MEAL NO. 2

**Spiced Beef Slices with
Dumplings**

Buttered Lima Beans   Cauliflower Salad
Raisin Bread Pudding

MEAL NO. 3

Devon Hashburgers

French Fried Potatoes   Assorted Relishes
Lettuce Wedges with French Dressing
Butterscotch Brownies

Sauerbraten American Style
with Noodles

The German favorite with an American accent!

6-pound rump roast of beef
1 tablespoon salt
½ teaspoon pepper
2 tablespoons dry mustard
6 tablespoons butter
1 cup minced onions
1 teaspoon oregano
1 bay leaf, crushed
¼ teaspoon ground sage
¼ teaspoon thyme

¾ cup tarragon vinegar
2 cans (6 ounces each) tomato paste
2 cups meat stock
3 carrots, finely chopped
½ cup celery leaves
¼ cup dry red wine
1 tablespoon cornstarch
2 tablespoons cold water
1 package (8 ounces) wide noodles, cooked

Wipe meat with damp cloth. Rub entire surface with mixture of salt, pepper, and dry mustard. Melt butter in a 5-quart Dutch oven or heavy skillet; add onions and sauté until lightly browned. Add meat; brown on all sides. Remove meat from Dutch oven. Add oregano, bay leaf, sage, thyme, tarragon vinegar, tomato paste, meat stock, carrots, and celery leaves. Bring to a boil. Place meat on a rack in Dutch oven. Cover tightly; simmer gently about 3½ hours or until meat is fork tender, turning meat 3 or 4 times. Add wine during last 30 minutes of cooking.

When meat is done, remove from pan and keep warm. Thicken sauce with cornstarch mixed with cold water. Cook sauce, stirring constantly, 5 minutes. Turn cooked noodles onto a heated platter. Slice meat and arrange attractively in center of platter. Pour some sauce over all. Serve remaining sauce separately. Makes 6 servings, with meat left over.

Spiced Beef Slices with Dumplings

I discovered this recipe in Bavaria and adapted it to American tastes.

½ cup vinegar
2 cups water
10 cloves
3 bay leaves
8 gingersnaps
1 tablespoon sugar
½ teaspoon salt
½ teaspoon Worcestershire sauce

6 slices sauerbraten
2 packages (4 envelopes) instant mashed potatoes
¼ cup flour
2 eggs, well beaten
½ teaspoon salt
⅛ teaspoon white pepper
¾ cup buttered crumbs

Combine the vinegar, water, cloves, bay leaves, gingersnaps, sugar, salt, and Worcestershire sauce in a large saucepan; bring to a boil, stirring until smooth. Add beef slices; heat gently 4 minutes. Set aside. To make the dumplings, prepare instant mashed potatoes according to package directions, but use ½ the liquid called for. Beat in the flour and eggs. Season with salt and white pepper. Shape into 6 dumplings. Drop into boiling water and cook until dumplings rise, about 8 to 10 minutes. Sprinkle dumplings with buttered crumbs and serve with hot beef slices. Makes 6 servings.

Devon Hashburgers

The original English countryside dish was served with buttered noodles, generously sprinkled with English Cheddar.

2 cups leftover sauerbraten, chopped	4 slices processed American cheese
⅓ cup chili sauce	4 black olives, pitted
⅓ cup sliced stuffed olives	1 tablespoon chopped parsley
4 English muffins	¼ teaspoon paprika

Preheat broiler 10 minutes. Combine chopped meat, chili sauce and stuffed olives. Split English muffins; toast split sides lightly. Spread with hash mixture; place under broiler just long enough to heat hash slightly. Top each muffin with a slice of cheese, quartering each slice to fit on muffin. Broil until cheese melts. Press a black olive into cheese on each muffin; sprinkle with paprika. Serve at once. Makes 4 servings.

RUMP OR CHUCK ROAST

A good rump or chuck roast of beef is always a welcome first meal. Here we offer an unusually flavored Flemish roast, a delightful Greek beef and onion dish, and to complete the international flavor, French Salmis of Beef. Buy a 7-pound roast and have the butcher cut off a 2-pound piece.

MEAL NO. 1

Flemish Roast

Potato Puffs   Creamed Cauliflower

Romaine Salad

Lord Baltimore Cake

MEAL NO. 2

Greek Stiffado

Whipped Potatoes   Julienne Carrots
Tossed Green Salad
Pistachio Ice Cream

MEAL NO. 3

French Salmis of Beef

Potatoes au Gratin   Buttered String Beans
Watercress Salad
Chocolate Pots de Crème

Flemish Roast

5-pound rump or chuck roast of beef
1 teaspoon ground coriander
1 teaspoon pepper
½ teaspoon red hot sauce
1½ tablespoons flour
2 tablespoons margarine
1½ cups beer
4 large onions, thinly sliced
2 cloves garlic, minced

1 tablespoon minced parsley
2 tablespoons butter
2 tablespoons vegetable oil
1½ teaspoons sugar
¾ teaspoon salt
½ teaspoon thyme
½ teaspoon sage
2 tablespoons chopped parsley

Rub roast with mixture of coriander, pepper, and hot sauce. Dust generously with flour. Melt margarine in a deep, heavy pan; brown meat on all sides. Add beer, bring to a boil; reduce heat, cover, and simmer 1½ hours. Sauté onions, garlic, and parsley in mixture of butter and oil. Add sugar and continue cooking until onions are light brown. Season with salt. Add onion mixture to meat, and sprinkle with thyme and sage. Cover, cook 1½ hours longer, or until meat is tender. Remove to a heated platter. Skim fat off sauce in pan. Spoon sauce over meat. Sprinkle with parsley. Makes 6 servings with leftovers.

Greek Stiffado

A traditional dish served throughout Greece and Turkey.

2 pounds rump or chuck roast
½ teaspoon salt
⅛ teaspoon pepper
1 tablespoon olive oil
1 onion, chopped
2 cloves garlic, finely chopped
4 tablespoons dry red wine
4 cups boiling water
1 tablespoon whole mixed spices
20 small white onions, peeled

1 tablespoon flour
¼ cup water
1 cup canned tomatoes
½ cup tomato sauce
1 teaspoon salt
¼ teaspoon pepper
4 bay leaves
⅓ cup wine vinegar
½ cup dry red wine

Cut meat into serving-size pieces; sprinkle with salt and pepper and set aside. Heat oil in a heavy skillet. Add chopped onion and garlic and sauté until golden brown. Add meat and brown on all sides. Add wine and boiling water. Tie spices in cheesecloth; add to meat. Cover; simmer 2 hours. Steam onions in water until just cooked. In a medium saucepan combine flour with water; gradually add remaining ingredients, stirring constantly until smooth. Cook 10 minutes, stirring. Skim fat from skillet. Add onions. Pour sauce over all gently. Cover; cook 25 minutes. Remove spice bag and serve. Makes 6 servings.

French Salmis of Beef

A party mixer so elegant to serve and so easy to make.

6 slices leftover Flemish Roast
2 tablespoons butter
2 tablespoons flour
¾ cup consommé

1 teaspoon lemon juice
½ cup dry red wine
1 teaspoon Worcestershire sauce

Trim meat slices. Melt butter in a large, heavy skillet, blend in flour, and cook 1 minute. Stir in consommé. Add lemon juice, wine, and Worcestershire sauce; stir until well blended and smooth. Add slices of meat. Spoon sauce over meat; cover, heat thoroughly over medium heat but do not boil. Makes 6 servings.

RIB ROAST

Entertaining? There's nothing more elegant than a handsome rib roast large enough for eight servings. Have the butcher cut off the short ribs and reserve them for an unusual family meal.

MEAL NO. 1

Peppered Rib Roast Americana

Twice-baked Potatoes
Broccoli Spears with Hollandaise
Cabbage—Carrot Slaw
Dutch Apple Pie

MEAL NO. 2

Fruited Short Ribs Italiano

Stewed Dried Lima Beans
Brussels Sprouts
Black Olive and Onion Salad
Date Bars

MEAL NO. 3

Western-style Beef

Mashed Potatoes   Glazed Carrots
Tossed Green Salad
Pickles
Sliced Pears and Oranges

Peppered Rib Roast Americana

3- or 4-rib roast of beef, about
  8 pounds
2 teaspoons pepper
1½ teaspoons salt

½ cup consommé
1½ tablespoons flour
3 tablespoons water

Heat oven to 400°F. Rub pepper and salt over top of roast. Set in a roasting pan; bake 45 minutes or until top has crusted lightly. Reduce heat to 350°F; bake 2 hours longer or to desired doneness, adding consommé during last hour and basting frequently with pan drippings. When done, remove to a heated platter. Skim off fat from pan drippings; make paste with flour and water, add to pan drippings, and stir until well-blended. Heat thoroughly and serve. Makes 6 servings.

Fruited Short Ribs Italiano

½ package (8-ounce size) mixed dried fruit
1½ cups boiling water
1¼ teaspoons paprika
1 teaspoon salt
¼ teaspoon pepper

short ribs cut from rib roast
4 medium potatoes, pared, cut in wedges
8 small onions, peeled
2 carrots, chopped
1 tablespoon chopped parsley

Place fruit in a bowl; pour boiling water over and let stand. Combine paprika, salt, and pepper. Rub mixture into short ribs. Brown ribs in a heated, heavy skillet. Add ½ cup water from fruit, cover, and simmer 1½ hours. Add potatoes, onions, and carrots and simmer 30 minutes. Drain fruit, reserving liquid. Add fruit to meat mixture; simmer 15 minutes, or until meat is tender, adding more fruit liquid, if necessary. Sprinkle with parsley. Makes 4 servings.

Western-style Beef

8 thin slices leftover roast beef
2 tablespoons butter
1 cup chopped onions
¼ cup chopped celery
1 tablespoon flour
1 cup consommé

¼ cup leftover roast beef gravy
½ cup tomato sauce
¾ teaspoon salt
¼ teaspoon pepper
¼ cup dry bread crumbs
1 tablespoon margarine

Heat oven to 450°F. Lay slices of meat in a heatproof dish, overlapping them slightly. Melt butter in a skillet. Add onions and celery and sauté until just light brown, stirring frequently. Blend in flour and stir until smooth. Add consommé and gravy; stir. Add tomato sauce, stirring constantly until thickened. Season with salt and pepper. Pour sauce over meat. Sprinkle with bread crumbs; dot with margarine. Bake 10 to 15 minutes. Makes 4 servings.

CHOPPED BEEF

Who can resist a "special" on chopped meat? But you don't have to serve hamburgers. Three pounds of chopped beef will give you three gourmet dishes from three different countries. Try them all and see!

MEAL NO. 1

Mexican Chilis Rellenos

Whipped Potatoes
Cucumber and Tomato Salad
Fruit Cocktail

MEAL NO. 2

Danish Meat Balls

French Fried Potatoes
Buttered Peas
Apple, Orange, and Onion Salad
Sour Cream Cake

MEAL NO. 3

Arabian Hamburger Kebabs

Herbed Rice
Grapefruit and Avocado Salad
Caramel Custard

Mexican Chilis Rellenos

In Mexico they serve these green peppers on feast days.

5 medium green peppers	1 teaspoon oregano
¼ cup olive oil	¼ cup finely chopped peanuts
1 pound ground beef	2 teaspoons flour
¼ cup canned tomato paste	½ cup vegetable oil
2 cloves garlic, minced	1 can (1 pound, 1 ounce) red
3 teaspoons chili powder	beans, heated
1 teaspoon salt	2 tomatoes, cut in wedges

Cut around stem of each green pepper. Gently pull out seeds and pulp with fingers and discard. Put peppers in a saucepan, add enough salted boiling water to cover, and cook 5 minutes. Drain and let cool 5 minutes. Heat olive oil in a skillet and add beef, tomato paste, garlic, chili powder, salt, oregano, and peanuts. Sauté mixture over low heat, stirring constantly, for

6 minutes. Cool slightly. Stuff peppers with mixture and lightly sprinkle with flour. Heat vegetable oil in a skillet. Fry peppers in oil, turning them once, until browned on all sides. Cover; cook 15 minutes. Put peppers in a ring on a serving platter, with heated red beans in the center. Garnish with tomato wedges. Serve hot. Makes 4 servings.

Danish Meat Balls

The most elegant of hot hors d'oeuvre.

1½ pounds ground beef	1 cup finely ground cracker crumbs
1 egg	¼ teaspoon pepper
1 teaspoon salt	½ cup commercial sour cream
2 tablespoons minced onion	2 tablespoons butter

Mix beef with all ingredients, except the butter. Blend well. Form into 24 small balls. Chill 4 hours. Fry in butter. Serve hot. Makes 6 to 8 servings.

Arabian Hamburger Kebabs

1 pound ground beef	1 small green pepper, cut into 8
½ teaspoon oregano	pieces
vegetable oil	4 thick slices sweet pickle
	8 mushroom caps

Mix beef with oregano and shape into 8 balls. Fry in oil for 5 minutes or until lightly browned. Put on skewers with pieces of green pepper, sweet pickle and mushroom caps. Brush with oil. Broil 10 to 15 minutes depending on desired doneness. Turn skewers over to cook kebabs evenly. Makes 4 servings.

TONGUE

From Switzerland comes a delightful tongue recipe to serve eight generously and have enough left over for two other meals.

MEAL NO. 1

Berneplatte

Sauerkraut with Caraway Seeds
Green Salad
Black Bread   Sweet Butter
Chocolate Parfait

MEAL NO. 2

Petits Tongue Rolls

Creamed Potatoes and Peas
Avocado and Grapefruit Salad on Bibb Lettuce
Tapioca Pudding with Fruit Sauce

MEAL NO. 3

Allah Stuffed Eggplant

Potato Pancakes   Tomato and Cucumber Salad
Heated Hard Rolls
Almond Cookies

Berneplatte

Whenever I visit a German rathskellar, I hope to find this tasty dish on the menu.

1 smoked beef tongue, about 6 pounds	2 sprigs parsley
4 bay leaves	8 lean short ribs of beef
2 teaspoons dried dill	1 pound ham hock
12 peppercorns	½ pound smoked sausage, cut in 1-inch pieces
10 whole allspice	2 pounds sauerkraut
1 medium onion, diced	1 teaspoon caraway seed
4 stalks celery, chopped	¼ teaspoon fennel seed

Cover tongue with cold water; bring to a boil, skimming the top occasionally. Boil vigorously 15 minutes. Discard water. Cover tongue with fresh boiling water. Add bay leaves, dill, peppercorns, allspice, onion, celery, and parsley. Simmer, uncovered, 1 hour, adding water as needed to keep tongue completely immersed in water. Remove tongue; strain stock and reserve. Cool tongue under running cold water, and strip off skin. Cut in half, reserving one half for other meals. Return one half to reserved stock in pot with short ribs, ham hock, and cut-up sausage. Cook 1½ hours or until all meats are tender. Drain sauerkraut and mix with caraway and fennel seeds; place in baking dish and bake at 325°F. 45 minutes or until thoroughly heated. Turn onto a heated platter; surround sauerkraut with slices of tongue, short ribs, cut-up ham hock, and sausage. Makes 8 servings.

Petits Tongue Rolls

Austrians serve leftover tongue in this gracious way.

12 small slices cooked tongue,
    sliced very thin
½ teaspoon chervil
1 teaspoon minced parsley
2 tablespoons minced green onions
½ teaspoon tarragon

1 teaspoon capers
½ teaspoon chopped gherkins
6 anchovies, mashed
4 slices crisp bacon, crumbled
1 tablespoon butter

Cut slices of cooked tongue on a slant; set aside. Heat oven to 450°F. Combine remaining ingredients, mashing them to a paste. Cut 12 6-inch squares of aluminum foil; grease lightly on one side. Lay tongue slices on foil. Spread mixture over them. Roll up each slice firmly, then roll foil around it, folding in ends and wrapping securely. Lay rolls close together, seam side down, in a 1-quart casserole. Bake 15 minutes. Unwrap on heated serving platter. Makes 4 servings.

Allah Stuffed Eggplant

A Near Eastern delicacy substituting tongue for the original goat's meat.

1 large eggplant
2 tablespoons olive oil
½ cup chopped celery
1 tablespoon minced parsley
3 mushrooms, chopped
¼ cup minced onion
1 cup lightly buttered bread crumbs

½ teaspoon chervil
¼ teaspoon marjoram
¼ teaspoon sage
1½ cups diced cooked tongue
½ teaspoon salt
⅛ teaspoon pepper
½ teaspoon paprika

Heat oven to 350°F. Cut the stem from the eggplant, trimming it carefully. Cut eggplant in half lengthwise. Parboil in boiling salted water 15 minutes, turning halves occasionally to cook evenly. Drain well. Scoop out pulp leaving ⅜-inch wall all around. Chop pulp coarsely; set aside. Heat oil in a skillet; add celery, parsley, mushrooms, and onion and sauté until lightly browned. Add eggplant pulp; sauté 3 minutes. Remove from heat. Stir in half the bread crumbs, the chervil, marjoram, sage, tongue, salt, and pepper; blend well. Heap mixture onto eggplant shells. Top with remaining bread crumbs. Place in a greased, shallow baking dish. Add 1½ tablespoons water and bake 30 minutes. To serve, cut with sharp knife lengthwise and serve shell and stuffing. Makes 4 servings.

LAMB

CROWN ROAST OF LAMB

A crown roast of lamb will make a spectacular entrée for company and give you two more meals which will make you happy there are leftovers. Have the butcher put together enough racks of lamb to make a crown weighing 8 to 10 pounds. He should also remove the chine, cut the ribs, tie the crown, and furnish you with paper frills for the bone ends. Be sure to give him a few days advance notice to prepare this.

MEAL NO. 1

Crown Roast of Lamb Niçoise

Potatoes Anna   Curried Broccoli

Raw Mushroom and Bibb Lettuce Salad

Chocolate Eclairs

MEAL NO. 2

Deviled Roast Lamb Bones

French Fried Potatoes

Watercress and Tomato Salad

Spumoni   Almond Cookies

MEAL NO. 3

Lamb Custard

Minted Peas   Boiled Carrots

Lettuce Wedges with Herb Mayonnaise

Lincoln Logs

Crown Roast of Lamb Niçoise

When I visited France I found out that this recipe called for a whole hot-house lamb. This is a young, unweaned sheep which has never grazed.

crown roast of lamb, 8 to 10 pounds
1½ teaspoons salt
¼ teaspoon pepper
1 teaspoon thyme
4 large carrots, diced
2 medium onions, diced
3 stalks of celery, diced

2 cloves garlic, minced
½ teaspoon sage
2 bay leaves
½ teaspoon rosemary
1 cup white wine
1½ cups consommé

Heat oven to 300°F. Wipe roast with damp cloth. Rub with salt, pepper, and thyme. Place in a shallow roasting pan; bake 2 hours. Add vegetables and herbs to pan; bake 45 minutes. [Total roasting time should be 30 minutes per pound.] Remove meat from pan to a heated platter. Skim fat off pan drippings, leaving vegetables in pan. Add wine and consommé. Boil vigorously 15 minutes. Strain, pressing vegetables through the strainer. Serve sauce with meat. Makes 8 servings.

Deviled Roast Lamb Bones

leftover lamb bones from
  cooked crown roast of lamb
2 teaspoons dry English mustard
½ cup water

½ cup bread crumbs
½ cup sherry
¼ cup prepared Dijon mustard
1½ cups lamb gravy

Leave a generous amount of meat on bones, cutting off remaining meat to make 1 cup for Lamb Custard. Combine English mustard with water; dip lamb bones into mixture. Coat bones with bread crumbs; place in a shallow baking pan. Broil 3 inches from source of heat, turning occasionally, until bones are brown, about 7 minutes. Place on a serving dish and keep hot. Heat wine over moderate heat and cook 1 minute. Add Dijon mustard and simmer 5 minutes. Add lamb gravy and heat thoroughly. Spoon sauce over bones and serve. Makes 4 servings.

Lamb Custard

Here's an instant gourmet meal which will delightfully surprise your friends.

1 cup cooked macaroni
1 cup finely chopped cooked lamb
½ teaspoon salt
⅛ teaspoon celery salt
⅛ teaspoon garlic salt
½ teaspoon minced parsley

½ teaspoon Angostura bitters
1 teaspoon minced onion
1 cup milk
½ cup light cream
2 eggs, lightly beaten
¼ cup grated Romano cheese

Heat oven to 350°F. Spread macaroni in a well-greased 1½-quart baking dish. Combine lamb with seasonings and onion. Arrange in a layer over macaroni. Combine milk, cream, and eggs and pour over meat. Bake 25 minutes. Sprinkle with cheese. Bake 5 minutes longer or until firm. Makes 4 servings.

SHOULDER OF LAMB—ONE

There are so many variations for a shoulder of lamb that you will soon make it a habit of having planned-over or leftover meats which will not only save you money, but also produce imaginative meals.

Have the butcher bone a 4- to 4½-pound shoulder of lamb. Save the bones for stock. Have 1½ pounds of meat ground.

MEAL NO. 1

Savory Stuffed Shoulder of Lamb

Creamed Onions   Succotash
Raw Spinach and Egg Salad
Spiced Pineapple Chunks
Vanilla Cookies

MEAL NO. 2

Lundi Lamb Casserole

Rice with Garbanzos   Sautéed Parsnips
Assorted Condiments
Cherry Pie

MEAL NO. 3

Mainland Meat Pie

Mashed Potatoes with Sesame Seeds
Creamed Cauliflower
Carrot Slaw
Fruit Cocktail

Savory Stuffed Shoulder of Lamb

3-pound boned shoulder of lamb
½ pound ground lamb
1 egg, well beaten
3 cups soft bread crumbs
2 tablespoons dry bread crumbs
2 tablespoons chopped onions
2 tablespoons chopped parsley

2 tablespoons fresh chopped mint leaves
3 tablespoons butter, melted
½ teaspoon salt
¼ teaspoon pepper
¼ teaspoon paprika
2 tablespoons tomato paste
1 teaspoon water

Heat oven to 350°F. Wipe meat with a damp cloth. Combine ground lamb, egg, all the bread crumbs, onions, parsley, and mint leaves to make the stuffing. Mix well. Spread mixture on shoulder of lamb. Roll and tie lamb securely with string. Brush with butter; season with salt, pepper, and paprika. Pour tomato paste diluted with water over meat. Place in a roasting pan; bake 1½ hours, basting occasionally, or until tender. Remove lamb from pan; cut strings and slice. Place slices on a heated platter, pour gravy over, and serve. Makes 6 servings.

Lundi Lamb Casserole

The blend of spices and tangy apples give this all-in-one meal its unusual flavor.

2 cups diced cooked lamb
¾ cup cooked stuffing
2 tablespoons butter
2 medium onions, coarsely chopped
2 small green apples, pared, cored, sliced
1 tablespoon curry powder
½ teaspoon coriander

1 tablespoon lemon juice
1 teaspoon sugar
½ teaspoon salt
¼ teaspoon pepper
1 cup consommé
¼ cup milk
1 tablespoon flour
1 tablespoon water

Heat oven to 350°F. Combine lamb and stuffing in a 1-quart baking dish. Heat butter in a medium, heavy skillet. Add onions and sauté until transparent. Add apples, curry powder, coriander, lemon juice, sugar, seasonings, consommé, and milk. Mix well. Turn into the baking dish. Cover; bake 35 minutes. Combine flour and water to make a paste. Stir into the sauce; bake 5 minutes. Makes 6 servings.

Mainland Meat Pie

1 tablespoon butter	2 tablespoons tomato sauce
1/2 cup finely chopped onion	2 cups lamb broth
1 pound ground lamb	4 slices dry toast
1/2 teaspoon salt	2 cups milk
1/8 teaspoon pepper	4 eggs, well beaten
1/8 teaspoon paprika	1/2 cup grated Parmesan cheese
1/2 teaspoon parsley	1 package pie crust mix
1 teaspoon cinnamon	melted butter

Melt the 1 tablespoon butter in a large, heavy skillet. Add onion and sauté until limp. Add ground meat and brown well. Drain off fat. Add seasonings, parsley, cinnamon, tomato sauce, and lamb broth. Cover and simmer 45 minutes. Soak toast in milk to soften. Mash to a soft paste; add to meat sauce, blending well. Combine eggs with cheese. Prepare pie crust mix according to package directions. Heat oven to 350°F. Line bottom of an 8 x 8 x 2-inch baking dish with half the pie crust; spread meat sauce over pastry. Cover with egg and cheese mixture. Cover with remaining pie crust. Brush crust with melted butter. Cut slits on top of pie crust. Bake 45 minutes. Remove pie from oven; let stand 12 minutes before cutting. Makes 6 servings.

SHOULDER OF LAMB—TWO

A lamb shoulder can yield many tempting meals. Plan on a 7- to 8-pound shoulder. Have the butcher bone it, and save the bones; then cut the meat into 2-inch cubes. Divide into three portions. Wrap separately and freeze, if desired, until needed.

MEAL NO. 1

Lamb de Provence

Buttered Noodles   Peas and Onions
Apple, Banana, and Date Salad
Coffee Ice Cream

MEAL NO. 2

Lamb Italiano

Fluffy Rice   Buttered Asparagus
Onion and Celery Salad
Prune Whip with Custard Sauce

MEAL NO. 3

Greek Lamb with Avgolemono Sauce

Artichoke Hearts   Baked Potatoes
Tossed Green Salad
Marble Pound Cake

Lamb de Provence

White vermouth and herbs add piquancy to this Continental dish.

2½ to 3 pounds boned shoulder of lamb, cut into 2-inch cubes	¼ teaspoon thyme
	¼ teaspoon sage
3 tablespoons vegetable oil	2 bay leaves
lamb bones	2 cups dry white vermouth
2 cups minced onions	3 cups beef bouillon
3 cloves garlic, minced	¾ cup water
1 tablespoon minced celery	¾ teaspoon salt
6 tablespoons tomato paste	¼ teaspoon pepper

Brown lamb cubes in hot vegetable oil in a large, heavy skillet. Remove lamb cubes. Add bones and brown well; remove bones, add onions and brown lightly. Drain fat from skillet. Add meat and bones. Add garlic, celery, tomato paste, thyme, sage, bay leaves, vermouth, bouillon, and water; blend well. Bring to a boil: reduce heat, season with salt and pepper, cover, and simmer 1½ hours. Discard bones and bay leaves, skim off fat, and serve. Makes 6 servings.

Lamb Italiano

A quick and easy leftover meal with lots of flavor.

2 to 2½ pounds boned shoulder
   of lamb, cut into 2-inch cubes
1 pound Mozzarella cheese
1½ pounds tomatoes, sliced
2 tablespoons butter, melted

¾ teaspoon salt
⅛ teaspoon pepper
⅛ teaspoon paprika
⅛ teaspoon oregano

Heat oven to 350°F. Place lamb in a 1½-quart baking dish. Cut cheese in small chunks and place on top of meat. Cover with tomatoes. Sprinkle with butter, salt, pepper, paprika, and oregano. Bake 1½ hours or until meat is tender. Makes 6 servings.

Greek Lamb with Avgolemono Sauce

The famous Greek lemon sauce gives the lamb its special flavor.

about 3 pounds boned shoulder
   of lamb, cut into 2-inch cubes
2 tablespoons butter
1 chopped onion
½ cup white wine
4 cups boiling water
¾ teaspoon salt

½ teaspoon onion salt
¼ teaspoon white pepper
1 tablespoon flour
¼ cup cold water
2 cups hot stock
3 eggs
juice of 3 lemons

In a large, heavy skillet brown meat on all sides in butter; remove meat to platter. Add onion and sauté until tender but not browned. Drain off all fat. Add wine, cover, and simmer 5 minutes. Add meat and simmer 10 minutes longer. Add boiling water, salts, and white pepper. Cover and simmer 1½ to 2 hours or until meat is tender. Skim off fat. Make a paste of flour and cold water: add to hot stock and cook 5 minutes. Beat eggs 5 minutes or until thick. Continue beating vigorously while adding, alternately in very small quantities, the thickened hot stock and lemon juice. Drain meat; pour lemon sauce over meat and serve immediately. *Do not cover and do not reheat as sauce will curdle.* Makes 6 servings.

Note: To make stock, boil lamb bones with 1 onion, 1 small potato, 1 carrot and a sprig of parsley in water to cover for 1 hour. Strain; continue boiling until stock is reduced to 2 cups.

SHOULDER OF LAMB—THREE

A 5- to 6-pound boned and rolled lamb shoulder will serve you nicely with a roast, a chafing-dish lamb curry, and elegant lamb rolls good enough for an unexpected company meal.

MEAL NO. 1

Lamb alla Veneziana

Potato Puffs   Creamed Zucchini
Green Salad
Cream Puffs

MEAL NO. 2

Lamb a l'Indienne

Fluffy Rice   Exotic Condiments
Avocado and Grape Salad
Vanilla Pudding   Caramel Sauce

MEAL NO. 3

Lamb Rolls Waldorf

Macaroni au Gratin
Green Beans Amandine
Jellied Tomato Salad
Orange Sherbet

Lamb alla Veneziana

5- to 6-pound boned, rolled shoulder of lamb	¼ teaspoon pepper
	2 tablespoons butter
1 teaspoon salt	2½ to 3 cups dry red wine

Wipe meat roll with a damp cloth. Sprinkle with salt and pepper. In a heavy, deep kettle melt butter; add lamb and brown well on all sides. Add 1 cup of the wine; cover tightly and simmer 1 hour. Skim off fat. Heat another 1 cup wine, add to meat, and cook 1 hour longer. Skim off fat again. Heat and add remaining wine; cook 25 minutes longer. Test for doneness. If meat is not tender, add ½ cup more heated wine and continue cooking until tender. Makes 6 servings with leftovers.

Lamb a l'Indienne

Coconut, curry powder, and cloves are uniquely combined in this popular Indian dish.

2 cups diced cooked lamb
2 medium cooking apples, cored,
  pared, sliced
1 green pepper, chopped
2 medium onions, sliced
1 clove garlic, minced
2 tablespoons olive oil
2 tablespoons flour
1½ tablespoons curry powder
½ teaspoon salt

⅛ teaspoon marjoram
pinch thyme
1 cup consommé
½ cup dry red wine
juice and grated rind of 1 lemon
½ cup seedless raisins
2 whole cloves
¼ cup shredded coconut
2 tablespoons chopped pistachio
  nuts

Sauté lamb, apples, green pepper, onions, and garlic in olive oil in a large, heavy skillet until onions are soft and transparent. Remove meat; set aside. Blend into the skillet a mixture of flour, curry powder, salt, and herbs. Cook 5 minutes over low heat. Stir in consommé, wine, lemon juice and rind, raisins, and cloves. Cover and simmer over very low heat 20 to 25 minutes, stirring occasionally. Add sautéed meat, coconut, and pistachio nuts. Heat thoroughly, about 5 minutes. Makes 6 servings.

Lamb Rolls Waldorf

6 large, very thin slices cooked lamb
½ cup seasoned bread stuffing
½ cup leftover gravy
2 tablespoons butter

2 tablespoons currant jelly
¾ teaspoon salt
¼ teaspoon pepper
1 tablespoon capers

Heat oven to 400°F. Lamb slices should be thin enough to roll up. Place slices on a flat surface. Place a spoonful of stuffing on each; roll up, tie with string, or fasten with wooden picks. Place in a shallow, greased 1-quart baking dish. Heat gravy in a saucepan with butter and jelly; when jelly is dissolved, pour mixture over rolls. Season with salt and pepper. Sprinkle capers over rolls. Bake 15 minutes, basting several times. Makes 6 servings.

LEG OF LAMB—ONE

Lamb is one of the most versatile meats and the imaginative cook, when she clears the roast from the table, is already visualizing the other meals it will produce. For three generous meals buy a 10-pound leg of lamb. Have it cut in half. Bone one half of the leg, and do take the bones and clippings home for broth and to make gravy.

MEAL NO. 1

Roast Leg of Lamb

Pan-browned Potatoes   Green Beans Amandine
Mint Gelatin Salad
Strawberry Shortcake

MEAL NO. 2

Lamb Shishkebab

French Fried Potatoes
Relishes   Greek Salad
Apricots in Brandy

MEAL NO. 3

Lamb Frikadeller

Broccoli and Red Onion Salad
Red Cabbage
Bread Pudding with Cinnamon Cream

Roast Leg of Lamb

4- to 5-pound leg of lamb
2 cloves garlic, halved
1 teaspoon salt
¼ teaspoon pepper
3 tablespoons butter, melted
2 tablespoons lemon juice

1 onion, finely chopped
1 cup dry white wine
½ cup water
½ cup vegetable oil
18 small white potatoes, pared
sprigs of fresh mint

Heat oven to 325°F. Wipe lamb with damp cloth. Slit in four places and insert pieces of garlic. Season with salt and pepper. Combine butter with lemon juice; lightly brush over lamb. Place lamb in a roasting pan, add chopped onion, wine, and water. Cover and bake 2 hours. Uncover, increase heat to 375°F, and continue baking 1 hour, basting every 15 minutes. Transfer to a heated platter; cover and keep warm. In a medium skillet heat oil to sizzling. Add potatoes and fry until golden brown. Skim fat from baking pan; add potatoes to meat drippings. Bake; uncovered, 30 minutes or until tender. Arrange potatoes around lamb. Decorate with mint. Makes 6 servings.

Lamb Shishkebab

24 1½- to 2-inch lamb cubes
1 medium onion, diced
1 teaspoon salt
¼ teaspoon pepper
2 cloves garlic, minced
1 teaspoon oregano
1 teaspoon paprika
½ teaspoon dry mustard

½ cup olive oil
¾ cup red wine
12 white onions, peeled, parboiled 10 minutes
2 medium green peppers, cut in 1-inch cubes, parboiled 10 minutes
24 small mushrooms
12 cubes Canadian bacon

Place lamb cubes in an earthenware bowl. Combine diced onion, salt, pepper, garlic, oregano, paprika, dry mustard, olive oil, and red wine; blend well. Pour marinade over meat; toss cubes until well coated. Refrigerate at least 24 hours in marinade. Fill 6 12-inch skewers, arranging on each equal portions of lamb, vegetables, and Canadian bacon. Broil 3 to 4 inches from source of heat for 15 minutes, turning two or three times during cooking. Serve hot. Makes 6 servings.

Lamb Frikadeller

A quick Dutch treat of lamb patties.

2 cups chopped cooked lamb
½ pound sausage meat
1 large onion, chopped
6 double saltine crackers, crushed

1 egg, well beaten
½ teaspoon salt
6 spiced crab apples
watercress

Combine lamb, sausage meat, and onion: mix well. Soak saltines in a cup with water to cover for 2 minutes; drain well. Combine with meat. Mix in egg and salt. Shape into 6 patties and brown slowly in a greased skillet 30 minutes, turning occasionally. Serve with crab apples and watercress. Makes 6 servings.

LEG OF LAMB—TWO

Here is another three-meal version of a leg of lamb using a 7- to 9-pound whole leg. Cut chops from the top of the leg for four servings, roast the remainder of the leg in paper, Continental Style, and serve Lamb Scallopini from the leftovers.

MEAL NO. 1

Lamb Breezoles

Rice Pilaf cooked in Lamb Broth
Parslied Carrots
Green Salad with Bleu Cheese Dressing
Apple Pie

MEAL NO. 2

Leg of Lamb Continental Style

Pan Fried Potatoes
Peas and Olives   Mint Jelly
Tossed Salad
Marble Cake with Ice Cream

MEAL NO. 3

Lamb Scallopini

Buttered Noodles
Okra with Tomatoes
Avocado and Onion Salad
Raspberry Gelatin

Lamb Breezoles

The Athenians like lemon juice generously squeezed over the lamb chops.

4 lamb chops, ¼ to ½ inch thick, cut from leg of lamb	1 teaspoon salt
¼ cup butter, melted	¼ teaspoon pepper
2 tablespoons lemon juice	½ teaspoon oregano
	½ teaspoon thyme

Broil lamb chops 3 to 4 inches from source of heat. Combine remaining ingredients. When chops begin to sizzle brush generously with butter mixture. Turn, brush other side and broil. Continue brushing and turning until done. Medium-done requires 12 minutes for both sides. Makes 4 servings.

Leg of Lamb Continental Style

leg of lamb with chops removed
3 cloves garlic, sliced
½ lemon
1 teaspoon salt

½ teaspoon pepper
½ cup grated Romano cheese
butter

Heat oven to 325°F. Wipe lamb with damp cloth. Cut slits into lamb and insert garlic slices. Rub lamb with lemon; sprinkle with salt, pepper, and cheese. Wrap leg of lamb in heavy cooking paper, closing both ends of paper together. Smear paper with butter. Place lamb in a roasting pan. Bake 1½ hours. Remove pan from oven; carefully remove paper and return lamb to pan. Increase oven heat to 375°F; bake 35 minutes or until done. Makes 4 servings with leftovers.

Lamb Scallopini

2 cups cooked lamb, cut in 1½-inch cubes
2 tablespoons butter
2 medium onions, sliced
1 small clove garlic, minced
2 small green peppers, sliced
¼ cup chopped celery

1 cup leftover lamb gravy
¼ cup red wine
½ teaspoon salt
¼ teaspoon pepper
2 tablespoons sherry
1 tablespoon minced parsley

Remove fat from lamb cubes. Heat butter in a medium skillet to sizzling; add onion, garlic, green peppers, and celery and lightly brown, stirring constantly. Blend in gravy and red wine. Season with salt and pepper. Add lamb cubes; stir gently, cover, and heat almost to boiling over low heat. Add sherry and stir. Sprinkle with parsley and serve. Makes 4 servings.

LEG OF LAMB—THREE

Buy a 7- to 9-pound leg of lamb. Have the butcher cut 2 lamb steaks about 1 inch thick from the center. Use thicker half for Roast Half Leg of Lamb. Reserve remaining meat uncooked for a third meal. Cook bones and reserve stock for gravy.

MEAL NO. 1

Roast Half Leg of Lamb

Roast Potatoes
Buttered Carrots with Mint
Grapefruit and Avocado Salad
Floating Island Custard

MEAL NO. 2

English Lamb Steaks

*Ginger Rice   Buttered Asparagus
Tossed Salad with Pistachio Nuts
Cheese Cake

MEAL NO. 3

Lamb à la Polsk

Mashed Potatoes   Minted Peas
Raw Spinach Salad
Sliced Peaches   Sponge Cake

Roast Half Leg of Lamb

½ leg of lamb (3 to 3½ pounds)   1 small onion, sliced
garlic powder   ½ cup water
salt

Heat oven to 350°F. Pierce lamb in about 6 places with skewers; fill holes with garlic powder. Rub salt over meat; place meat in a roasting pan. Add onion and water around lamb. Cover; roast until done to taste, 30 minutes per pound for well done. Remove cover; roast 15 minutes longer, or until browned. Makes 4 servings.

English Lamb Steaks

2 lamb steaks, about 1 inch thick,   ½ teaspoon curry powder
   cut from half a leg of lamb   seeds from 1 cardamon pod, crushed
¾ cup canned pineapple juice   Ginger Rice (*see below*)
½ teaspoon ginger

Place steaks in a single layer in a shallow pan. Mix pineapple juice, ginger, curry powder, and crushed cardamon and pour over steaks. Cover; place in refrigerator for at least 12 hours, turning once. Drain; save marinade. Broil steaks, 4 inches from heat, 6 minutes on each side. Serve with Ginger Rice. Makes 4 servings.

Ginger Rice

pineapple-spice liquid marinade   1 teaspoon salt
water   1 cup rice

Measure pineapple-spice marinade from marinated lamb steaks and add enough water to make 2 cups liquid. Heat to boiling in a medium saucepan; stir in salt. Add rice; cover. Simmer 30 minutes or until rice is tender and liquid is absorbed. Makes 4 servings.

Lamb à la Polsk

This Polish recipe calls for a lamb shoulder with lots of sour cream, served with red cabbage.

2 cups leftover uncooked lamb	1 cup water
1¼ cups diced celery	1 cup commercial sour cream
3 medium carrots, scraped, thinly sliced	¼ cup chopped parsley
1 medium onion, chopped	2 tablespoons flour
1 small tomato, chopped	¾ teaspoon caraway seeds
1 teaspoon salt	1 cup biscuit mix
	6 tablespoons light cream

Heat oven to 375°F. Trim fat from lamb; cut lamb into cubes. Combine lamb with celery, carrots, onion, tomato, salt, and water in a 1½-quart pan. Cover tightly. Bake 1 hour or until meat is tender. Mix sour cream with parsley, flour, and caraway seeds in a small bowl. Combine biscuit mix and cream in a second bowl. Remove pan from oven; stir in sour-cream mixture. Drop biscuit dough from a teaspoon to make 8 mounds around edge of pan. Bake, uncovered, 15 to 20 minutes longer, or until biscuits are lightly browned. Makes 4 servings.

PORK AND HAM

FRESH HAM

A 5-pound fresh ham, shank end, is the inspiration for three unusual meals. Have the butcher cut off 2 pounds of meat, and cut it into 1½-inch cubes; have 1 pound of meat ground finely along with ⅓ pound of pork fat for the unusual homemade sausage cakes. The 2-pound piece is for Roast Fresh Ham.

MEAL NO. 1

Roast Fresh Ham with Apple Rings

Parslied Whipped Potatoes
Cabbage with Caraway Seeds
Butterscotch Pudding

MEAL NO. 2

Sweet Pork Ariadne

Buttered Broccoli Spears
Cherry Tomatoes and Hearts of Celery
Pineapple Pudding with Melba Sauce

MEAL NO. 3

Homemade Sausage Cakes Alexandra

Mashed Potatoes
String Beans with Almonds
Romaine Salad with Italian Dressing
Apple Pie

Roast Fresh Ham with Apple Rings

shank end of fresh ham (2 pounds)	1 teaspoon sage
¾ teaspoon celery salt	2 large apples, unpeeled, cored
⅛ teaspoon pepper	3 tablespoons shortening

Heat oven to 350°F. Rub ham with combined celery salt, pepper, and sage. Place in a roasting pan; roast, covered, 1½ hours. Uncover, continue roasting 30 minutes. Cut apples into rings and fry in shortening 2 minutes. Add apple rings to roasting pan; continue baking 25 minutes longer. Makes 4 servings.

Sweet Pork Ariadne

This is an adaptation of the Viennese favorite.

1½ cups boiling water
½ package (8 ounces) dried
   apricots
2 pounds boneless pork, cut in
   1½-inch cubes
1 tablespoon butter

2½ tablespoons soy sauce
dash Tabasco
⅛ teaspoon pepper
6 green onions, cut in 2-inch pieces
2 cups fluffy, cooked rice
1 tablespoon chopped parsley

Pour boiling water over apricots and let stand. Brown meat in butter in a medium, heavy skillet until well browned on all sides. Add soy sauce, Tabasco, pepper, and half the apricot liquid. Cover and simmer 45 minutes. Add onions, apricots, and more apricot liquid if necessary. Simmer 10 minutes longer, or until meat and apricots are tender. Serve over rice; sprinkle with parsley. Makes 6 servings.

Homemade Sausage Cakes Alexandra

This is a luxurious hors d'oeuvre.

2 cups ground pork
⅔ cup ground pork fat
1½ teaspoons salt
½ teaspoon celery salt
⅛ teaspoon pepper

dash allspice
dash mace
⅛ teaspoon crumbled bay leaf
1 small clove garlic, minced
¼ cup cognac

Combine all ingredients in a large mixing bowl. Beat mixture vigorously until well blended. Form into cakes 2 inches in diameter and ½ inch thick. Brown cakes lightly on both sides in a heavy skillet and cook until well done. Drain on absorbent towels. Makes 6 servings.

PORK LOIN

Buy a 5-pound, 12-chop pork loin. Have the butcher cut 6 thick chops from the rib end. Trim the remaining shoulder pieces from the bones. Cube meat and freeze, if desired, until needed for your second meal. Freeze the bones, or prepare soup and freeze it until needed.

MEAL NO. 1

Pork Fruitadella

Spinach Soufflé   Parslied Carrots
Tomato and Cucumber Salad
Pears with Lemon Velvet Sauce

MEAL NO. 2

Pork Mexicano

Succotash Amandine
Spicy Cole Slaw
Ice Cream Cake

MEAL NO. 3

Minnesota Pea Soup

Glazed Canadian Bacon
Sesame Toast
Double Chocolate Cake

Pork Fruitadella

6 thick pork chops from rib end of
   pork roast
½ teaspoon salt
¼ teaspoon pepper
dash of mace
2 large oranges

2 tablespoons brown sugar
⅛ teaspoon nutmeg
5 slices white bread, diced
½ cup whole-cranberry sauce
¼ teaspoon onion salt

Heat oven to 350°F. Trim excess fat from chops and place it in a large, heavy skillet. Heat until a small amount of liquid fat coats skillet; discard trimmings. Sprinkle chops with salt, pepper, and mace and brown them in the skillet. Remove chops and arrange in a single layer in a shallow baking dish.

Cut 6 even-size slices from middle of oranges and set aside. Squeeze juice from remaining pieces and add water, if necessary, to make ½ cup liquid. Stir in brown sugar and nutmeg and blend. Pour mixture over chops. Bake 45 minutes, basting occasionally. Mix diced bread, cranberry sauce, and onion salt in a small bowl; divide mixture evenly into mounds on the 6 orange slices and set on top of chops. Spoon juices from pan over all. Bake chops 15 minutes longer. Makes 6 servings.

Pork Mexicano

2 to 2½ pounds uncooked shoulder-end pork roast
1 large onion, sliced
1 can (1 pound) tomatoes
1 can (8 ounces) tomato sauce
¼ cup diced celery
¼ cup chopped parsley
1 teaspoon salt
1 teaspoon sugar
½ teaspoon chili powder
⅛ teaspoon pepper
⅛ teaspoon paprika
½ cup sliced stuffed green olives
1 package (8 ounces) noodles, cooked, drained, seasoned

Cut meat from bones and save bones for soup. Trim off fat and cube meat. Sauté meat and onion in a heavy, dry skillet until meat is lightly browned. Stir in tomatoes, tomato sauce, celery, parsley, salt, sugar, chili powder, pepper, and paprika. Heat mixture to boiling. Cover skillet, reduce heat, and simmer 1 hour or until meat is tender. Stir in olives and cook 5 minutes longer. Serve with hot noodles. Makes 6 servings.

Minnesota Pea Soup

A hearty soup for those cold winters, simmered to a perfect blend of flavors.

1 package (1 pound) split green peas
leftover uncooked pork bones
½ cup diced celery
¼ cup diced onion
½ cup diced carrots
¼ cup chopped green onions
1 bay leaf
1 tablespoon salt
¼ teaspoon pepper
5 cups water
4 cups canned mixed vegetable juice

Combine peas, pork bones, celery, onion, carrots, green onions, bay leaf, salt, pepper, water, and 2 cups of the vegetable juice in a large, heavy kettle; bring to a boil. Reduce heat and simmer, stirring occasionally, for 2 hours or·until peas are mushy. Remove pork bones and bay leaf. Cut off any lean meat from bones and return it to soup. Stir in remaining 2 cups vegetable juice. Heat just to boiling and serve. Makes 8 to 10 cups.

SMOKED PORK SHOULDER

A simmered smoked pork shoulder is hearty family fare. It cooks ever so tender and is truly a no-fuss meal. For the planned second and third meals we feature a golden soufflé and a sherried casserole which are elegant enough for company fare.

MEAL NO. 1

Simmered Smoked Pork Shoulder

Boiled Potatoes
Harvard Beets
Cole Slaw
Baked Apples with Honey

MEAL NO. 2

Golden Pork Soufflé

Creamy Mashed Potatoes
Cranberried Carrot Slivers
Crisp Spinach and Radishes
Eclairs

MEAL NO. 3

Sherried Pork Casserole

Buttered Noodles
Broccoli with French Dressing
Mixed Green Salad
Coconut Cream Pie

Simmered Smoked Pork Shoulder

5- to 6-pound smoked pork
   shoulder
1 large onion

3 whole cloves
1 tablespoon brown sugar
1 celery stalk, cut up

Place meat in a large, heavy saucepan. Add water to cover; add onion stuck with cloves, brown sugar, and celery. Bring to a boil, reduce heat, and simmer 1½ hours or until meat is tender. When done, remove meat to a heated platter. Discard onion with cloves and celery. Reduce liquid to half by boiling; use as is, or thicken with flour paste for a sauce. Makes 6 servings.

Golden Pork Soufflé

The substantial smoked pork is a surprise ingredient in this delicate dish.

½ cup butter
6 eggs, separated
2 cups grated Parmesan cheese
2 tablespoons finely chopped chives

1 cup cooked, chopped,
   smoked pork
1 tablespoon finely chopped parsley

Heat oven to 350°F. Cream butter until soft; add egg yolks, one at a time, beating constantly, until mixture is light and fluffy. Add cheese, chives, pork, and parsley. Beat egg whites until stiff and fold into mixture. Pour into a well-greased 1-quart baking dish. Bake 30 to 35 minutes or until knife inserted near the center comes out clean. Makes 6 servings.

Sherried Pork Casserole

2 eggs, well beaten
½ cup heavy cream
1 teaspoon Worcestershire sauce
dash Tabasco
½ cup sherry
4 cups leftover smoked pork,
   ground

2 tablespoons diced green pepper
2 cups cooked rice
2 medium tomatoes, peeled,
   chopped
1 tablespoon grated onion
1 teaspoon prepared mustard
⅛ teaspoon thyme

Heat oven to 350°F. Combine eggs with cream, Worcestershire sauce, Tabasco, and wine; blend well. Combine all remaining ingredients except thyme. Add to egg mixture, blending well. Turn into a well-greased 1½-quart baking dish. Bake 45 minutes. Sprinkle thyme over the top during last 15 minutes of baking. Makes 6 servings.

READY-TO-EAT HAM—ONE

Bake a big ham and the good eating has just begun, for there are so many ways to turn second-day servings into second-day bests.

MEAL NO. 1

Ham with Pineapple Glaze

Tomato Rice   Squash with Almonds
Mustard Sauce
Spring Salad
Orange Cake

MEAL NO. 2

Pineapple Upside-Down Delight

Mashed Sweet Potatoes
Red Cabbage
Crisp Green Salad
Chocolate Brownies

MEAL NO. 3

Ham Mousse Bordeaux

Fried Potato Puffs with Fennel
Caesar Salad
Cheese Cake

Ham with Pineapple Glaze

8- to 8½-pound ready-to-eat
  half ham
½ cup pineapple juice

1 cup brown sugar
2 tablespoons honey
⅛ teaspoon nutmeg

Heat oven to 325°F. Score top of ham with diagonal cuts, making diamonds. Place ham in a shallow baking dish; bake 1¼ hours. Combine remaining ingredients and spread mixture over ham. Increase oven heat to 400°F. Bake 30 minutes longer, or until ham is well glazed. Makes 6 to 8 servings with leftovers.

Pineapple Upside-Down Delight

An old recipe of the Midwest known also as Cinderella's Meal.

1 small onion, chopped	½ teaspoon Tabasco
2 tablespoons butter	¼ teaspoon prepared mustard
2 cups ground cooked ham	¼ teaspoon salt
2 eggs, well beaten	⅛ teaspoon pepper
½ cup bread crumbs	1½ tablespoons margarine
1 tablespoon ketchup	2 tablespoons brown sugar
1 tablespoon chili sauce	3 slices canned pineapple
1½ teaspoons Worcestershire sauce	3 maraschino cherries

Heat oven to 350°F. Brown onion lightly in butter in a medium skillet. Combine with ham, eggs, bread crumbs, ketchup, chili sauce, Worcestershire sauce, Tabasco, prepared mustard, salt, and pepper. Melt margarine and sugar together and pour into a 9-inch square pan. Lay in the pineapple slices; place a cherry in center of each slice. Pile ham mixture on top. Bake 40 minutes. To serve, invert on a platter. Makes 6 servings.

Ham Mousse Bordeaux

A Cordon Bleu dish, streamlined for busy housewives.

1 tablespoon butter	1½ tablespoons unflavored gelatin
1 tablespoon flour	½ cup water
1 cup milk	2 cups cooked ham, cut in
½ teaspoon salt	julienne strips
1 small onion, minced	1 cup heavy cream, whipped
2 tablespoons margarine	watercress
1 teaspoon paprika	parsley
1 teaspoon soy sauce	

Combine butter, flour, milk, and salt in a small saucepan and cook, stirring constantly, until thickened. Cool. Cook onion in margarine in a medium saucepan until tender. Add cream sauce, paprika, and soy sauce; blend. Soak gelatin in water and dissolve over hot water. Stir into mixture. Stir in ham. Fold in whipped cream. Pour mixture into a 3-cup mold. Chill until firm. Unmold on a bed of watercress and parsley on a chilled platter. Makes 6 servings.

CANNED HAM

A canned cooked ham is an excellent buy as there is no waste. Plan the first meal as a culinary treat for your family or friends and let the planned-over second and third meals supply time-honored and delicious dinners.

MEAL NO.1

Baked Ham Lieges

Baked Potatoes with Sour Cream
Lima Bean Salad
Lime Sherbert

MEAL NO. 2

Ham Holiday Mold

French Fried Potatoes
Cauliflower and Anchovy Salad
Orange Sherbet with Bourbon

MEAL NO. 3

Ham In Port Wine Elias

*Pimiento Waffles
Crisp Green Salad
Date Nut Bars à la Mode

Baked Ham Lieges

1½ cups raisins
1½ cups boiling water
1 can (4 to 5 pounds) boneless cooked ham
2 tablespoons prepared mustard

1 teaspoon dry mustard
¼ teaspoon cumin
1 package (10 ounces) frozen Brussels sprouts
1 cup slightly cooked carrot slices

Place raisins in a bowl; pour water over them and let stand. Heat oven to 350°F. Place ham in a shallow baking pan; brush top and sides of ham with prepared mustard. Sprinkle with combined dry mustard and cumin. Arrange vegetables around ham. Add raisins and raisin liquid. Bake 45 to 55 minutes, basting frequently, adding more water if necessary. Makes 4 to 6 servings.

Ham Holiday Mold

The distinctive flavor comes from all the ingredients but mostly from the cider and horseradish.

1 cup seedless raisins
1 quart sweet cider
4 whole cloves
¼ cup brown sugar
2 envelopes unflavored gelatin
3 tablespoons water
1 tablespoon lemon juice
½ teaspoon salt

dash cayenne
pinch nutmeg
2¼ cups cooked ham, cut in
   julienne strips
2 cups mixed cooked vegetables
¼ cup mayonnaise
1 teaspoon prepared horseradish
1 tablespoon chopped parsley

Soak raisins in cider 30 minutes. Add cloves and brown sugar; heat mixture slowly to boiling. Remove from heat. Soak gelatin in combined water and lemon juice for 3 minutes. Add cider mixture and stir until gelatin is dissolved. Add salt, cayenne, and nutmeg. Chill until mixture begins to thicken. Stir in ham. Pour mixture into a 4-cup ring mold and chill until firm. Unmold on a chilled platter. Combine cooked vegetables with mayonnaise and horseradish and spoon into center of mold. Sprinkle with parsley. Makes 6 servings.

Ham in Port Wine Elias

Elias, the amiable maître d'hôtel of the Minos Hotel in Crete, shared this recipe with me.

3 tablespoons butter
2 cups cooked ham, cut in
   2-inch cubes
½ cup port wine
1 dash Angostura bitters

dash Worcestershire sauce
1½ cups heavy cream
pinch ground cloves
pinch nutmeg
Pimiento Waffles *(see below)*

Heat butter to almost sizzling point in a heavy skillet. Add ham and lightly sauté. Add wine, bitters, and Worcestershire sauce and simmer until half the liquid remains. Stir in cream, cloves, and nutmeg. Increase heat slightly and cook, stirring constantly, until sauce is thickened. Serve on Pimiento Waffles. Makes 4 to 6 servings.

Pimiento Waffles

2 cups sifted cake flour
2 teaspoons baking powder
½ teaspoon salt
2 egg yolks

1¼ cups milk
6 tablespoons vegetable oil
3 egg whites
3 tablespoons chopped pimiento

Preheat waffle iron. Combine flour, baking powder, and salt; set aside. In a medium bowl beat egg yolks, milk, and vegetable oil until well blended. Gradually add flour mixture, a little at a time, beating after each addition; beat only until smooth. In a small bowl, beat egg whites until stiff peaks form when beater is raised. Gently fold egg whites into batter just until combined. Stir in pimiento. For each waffle, pour batter into center of preheated waffle iron until it spreads to 1 inch from edge, about ½ cup. Cook to desired doneness, 4 to 5 minutes. Serve hot. Makes 4 to 6 waffles, depending on size of waffle iron.

READY-TO-EAT HAM—TWO

It has been argued that leftover meats can be used to make meals that have more excitement and savor than the original roasts. And many homemakers plan-over their extra meals not merely as a necessary economy but as real table luxuries. Half a ham can give generous servings for six to eight with at least three meals planned around the original roast.

MEAL NO. 1

Baked Ham à la Gregory

Scalloped Potatoes   Caraway Cabbage
Orange and Apple Salad
Sour Cream Cake

MEAL NO. 2

New Orleans Gumbo

Sesame French Bread Chunks
Chick Peas and Tossed Greens Salad
Blueberry Turnovers

MEAL NO. 3

Chinese Pork Curry

Hot Fluffy Rice   Applesauce with Mint
Fried Squash
Almond Cookies

Baked Ham à la Gregory

8- to 9-pound ready-to-eat
half ham, shank end
1 can (1 pound 14 ounces)
pitted Bing cherries
¼ cup honey
2 tablespoons cornstarch
¼ teaspoon cinnamon

⅛ teaspoon cloves
⅛ teaspoon mace
½ teaspoon dry mustard
½ teaspoon salt
2 tablespoons sugar
¼ cup sherry

Have butcher bone ham; save bones for another meal. Remove skin from top of ham. Stuff ham pocket formed by removing bones with drained cherries, reserving liquid and remaining cherries for sauce. Tie string around ham. Score top with diagonal cuts, making diamonds. Heat oven to 325°F. Place ham in a shallow baking dish and bake 1½ hours. Increase oven heat to 400°F. Drizzle honey over ham; bake ½ hour longer or until ham is glazed. Prepare sauce by stirring cornstarch, cinnamon, cloves, mace, mustard, salt, sugar, and wine into reserved cherry juice. Heat almost to boiling, add remaining cherries, and simmer 1 minute. Makes 6 to 8 servings with leftovers.

New Orleans Gumbo

In the elegant old-quarter restaurants, gumbos are varied but all are traditionally served with rice.

4 bacon strips
½ cup chopped green onions
1 clove garlic, minced
5 tablespoons flour
5 cups water
2½ teaspoons salt
½ teaspoon thyme
¼ teaspoon pepper
2 cans (1 pound each) whole
tomatoes, drained

2 bay leaves
1½ cups cooked ham, cut into
¾ -inch cubes
1 package (10 ounces) frozen okra
2 pounds uncooked medium shrimp,
peeled, deveined, split lengthwise
1 package (6 ounces) frozen
Alaska king crab meat
1¼ cups cooked hot rice

In a large, heavy skillet sauté bacon until crisp. Remove, chop coarsely and set aside. In bacon drippings, sauté green onions and garlic until tender. Sprinkle in flour and stir until blended. Gradually add water, stirring until smooth. Add salt, thyme, pepper, tomatoes, bay leaves, and ham. Cover and simmer 30 minutes, stirring occasionally. Cut okra in half and add. Cook 14 minutes. Add shrimp and crab meat and simmer, uncovered, 10 minutes or until shrimp are tender. Remove bay leaves. Sprinkle bacon bits over mixture. Serve in soup bowls, first spooning rice into each. Makes 8 servings.

Chinese Pork Curry

A mix of Oriental cuisines makes this a happy Hong Kong concoction.

¼ cup butter	¼ teaspoon pepper
1 large Bermuda onion, finely chopped	⅛ teaspoon thyme
	2 tablespoons curry powder
¼ teaspoon salt	2 cups chicken consommé
½ teaspoon celery salt	¾ cup heavy cream
⅛ teaspoon ground cloves	1½ tablespoons flour
⅛ teaspoon nutmeg	3 cups diced cooked lean pork

Melt butter in a heavy skillet; cook onion in butter until it begins to turn yellow. Add salts, cloves, nutmeg, pepper, thyme, and curry powder and simmer 15 minutes. Add consommé and simmer 10 minutes. Strain through a fine sieve into a large saucepan. Bring to a boil and gradually stir in cream. Stir in flour until smooth. Add meat. Cook slowly 15 to 20 minutes until thoroughly heated. Makes 8 servings.

FRESH HAM

A fresh ham is a welcome change in the winter. Have the butcher cut off two slices, each about ½ inch thick, for one meal and plan to serve the remainder with a succulent stuffing. The butcher will bone the ham for you and make a pocket for the stuffing.

MEAL NO. 1

Stuffed Fresh Ham Supreme

Mashed Potatoes   Brussels Sprouts
Lettuce Hearts with Roquefort Dressing
Fresh Berry Tarts

MEAL NO. 2

Mock Goose Trianon

Sweet Potato Pie   Eggplant Parmigiana
Grapefruit and Avocado Salad
Coffee Ice Cream

MEAL NO. 3

Pork and Stuffing Loaf

Noodles Romanoff   Fried Apple Rings
Endive and Watercress Salad
Pecan Pie

Stuffed Fresh Ham Supreme

A Mediterranean version with plump raisins in the stuffing.

5- to 6-pound fresh ham, boned
1 cup packaged savory stuffing
3 cups stale bread crumbs
1½ cups chopped onion
½ cup chopped celery
¼ cup butter, melted
¼ cup light cream

1 cup seedless raisins
1 teaspoon dried sage leaves
¾ teaspoon salt
⅛ teaspoon pepper
2 tablespoons flour
2 tablespoons water

Have butcher bone a fresh ham to make a pocket for stuffing. Heat oven to 350°F. Combine remaining ingredients, except flour and water; mix well. Stuff pocket of meat loosely with stuffing. Bake, covered, 1½ hours. Uncover, continue baking 1 hour longer or until meat is tender. Skim fat off drippings. Keep ham warm on a heated platter. Make gravy with a paste of flour and water. Makes 6 servings with leftovers.

Mock Goose Trianon

The original time-consuming recipe was a Trianon favorite—our version is quick, easy and tasty.

2 slices fresh ham, ½ inch thick
½ teaspoon salt
¼ teaspoon pepper
1 cup dried apple rings,
  soaked in water
4 maraschino cherries

2 tablespoons butter
1 jar (1 pound) sweet-sour
  red cabbage
1 tablespoon light brown sugar
1 teaspoon caraway seed

Pound meat slices thin and halve them lengthwise. Season with salt and pepper. Place 1 apple ring and 1 cherry on each, roll up, and secure with a wooden pick. Brown butter in a heavy skillet; add meat rolls and brown evenly on all sides. Mix cabbage, sugar, and caraway seed. Remove meat rolls from skillet. Arrange cabbage mixture in bottom of skillet. Top with meat rolls. Cover, bring to a boil, reduce heat and simmer 1 hour or until tender. Add water, if necessary. Remove wooden picks before serving. Makes 4 servings.

Pork and Stuffing Loaf

Intriguing enough for company. Especially good for informal buffet service.

4 cups coarsely ground cooked pork
1 cup packaged savory stuffing
¾ cup pork gravy
2 eggs, well beaten
1 can (5⅓ ounces) evaporated
  milk
½ cup chopped celery
¼ cup chopped green pepper

¼ cup chopped red pepper
1 small onion, minced
4 tablespoons butter, melted
¾ teaspoon salt
¼ teaspoon pepper
¼ cup dry bread crumbs
3 pimiento strips
1 tablespoon chopped parsley

Heat oven to 400°F. Combine pork, stuffing, gravy, eggs, evaporated milk, celery, green and red peppers, onion, 2 tablespoons of the butter, salt, and pepper. Pat into a greased 1½-quart loaf pan. Sprinkle with bread crumbs and remaining 2 tablespoons butter. Bake 45 minutes. Unmold on a heated platter. Garnish with pimiento strips and parsley. Makes 6 servings.

LOIN OF PORK

What remains of the roast can be the beginning of some excellent dishes. Many of the world's great traditional dishes were developed by cooks who found the cupboard not bare but full of leftovers. Inventively combining ingredients and improvising, they came up with new culinary triumphs.

Take a loin of pork, for instance, and have the butcher cut off 4 large pork chops from the lean end; plan the Roast Loin of Pork Island Style as your main meal, the Pork Chops Marseilles for a tasty supper, and any leftover cooked pork, cut in thin strips, will give you the exotic Chinatown Chop Suey.

MEAL NO. 1

Roast Loin of Pork Island Style

Potatoes au Gratin

Waldorf Salad   Cucumber Sticks

Fudge Cake

MEAL NO. 2

Pork Chops Marseilles

Rissole Potatoes   Fresh Asparagus

Chicory Salad

Angel Food Cake

MEAL NO. 3

Chinatown Chop Suey

Fried Egg Noodles

Tossed Greens

Ice Cream   Fortune Cookies

Roast Loin of Pork Island Style

1½ teaspoons salt
1 teaspoon whole allspice
½ teaspoon nutmeg
1 teaspoon ground cloves
½ teaspoon black pepper
½ teaspoon marjoram
½ teaspoon sage
½ teaspoon thyme
1 crumbled bay leaf
1 tablespoon grated lemon rind
2 tablespoons lemon juice

2½ cups consommé
2¼ cups water
6- to 6½-pound pork loin roast
3 cups cubed cooked carrots
12 small white onions, cooked
3 medium tomatoes
1 tablespoon chopped parsley
1 teaspoon celery salt
½ teaspoon paprika
½ teaspoon oregano

To make marinade, combine the first thirteen ingredients in a medium saucepan and bring to a boil. Cover, reduce heat and simmer 10 minutes. Cool. Place pork roast in a roasting pan and add marinade. Refrigerate one day, turning meat several times. Pour marinade into a bowl and reserve. Heat oven to 325°F. Roast pork uncovered, 2 hours. Add carrots and onions; pour marinade over all. Continue baking 45 minutes longer. Halve tomatoes, add to roasting pan, and sprinkle remaining 4 ingredients over them. Bake 15 minutes longer. Turn pork onto a heated platter. Arrange vegetables around meat, pour drippings over, and serve. Makes 6 servings.

Pork Chops Marseilles

The port of a thousand nationalities yielded this hearty dish.

1 cup dried apricots	1 teaspoon salt
¼ cup raisins	⅛ teaspoon pepper
boiling water	2 tablespoons butter
4 large pork chops	½ cup consommé
3 tablespoons flour	¼ cup brown sugar

Place apricots and raisins in a bowl; add boiling water to cover and let stand overnight. Force mixture through a sieve or purée in an electric blender. Coat pork chops with combined flour, salt, and pepper. Place in a shallow 2-quart baking pan; top with fruit purée. Pour consommé over all and bake 45 minutes, covered. Uncover; sprinkle with brown sugar. Bake, uncovered, 20 minutes longer or until chops are tender. Makes 4 servings.

Chinatown Chop Suey

½ cup water	¼ cup sliced water chestnuts
1 package frozen green beans, French style	1 large onion, sliced
1 cup frozen peas	1 cup bouillon
1 cup diced celery	3 tablespoons soy sauce
¼ cup frozen lima beans	1 can (1 pound) bean sprouts, drained
3 cups cooked pork, cut in thin strips	2 tablespoons cornstarch
¼ cup diced green pepper	2 tablespoons water
¼ cup diced red pepper	2 cups fried rice
	6 strips candied ginger

Bring ½ cup water to a boil in a large saucepan. Add green beans, peas, celery, and lima beans; cook 5 minutes. Add meat, green and red pepper,

water chestnuts, onion, cup of bouillon, soy sauce, and bean sprouts and
cook until liquid comes to a boil. Blend cornstarch with water and stir into
mixture. Cook until thickened. Serve with fried rice and ginger. Makes 6
servings.

VEAL

BREAST OF VEAL—ONE

Order an 8½-pound breast of veal and have butcher cut it into 3-pound,
3½-pound and 2-pound pieces. Have the first two pieces prepared for stuffing by cutting in a pocket. Have the 2-pound piece cut into 3-inch cubes.

MEAL NO. 1

Veal Del Mar

Green Beans with Almonds
Parslied New Potatoes
Sliced Tomatoes
Cherry Jubilee Meringue

MEAL NO. 2

Pennsylvania Dutch Veal

Creamed Carrots   Fried Potato Balls
Mixed Greens with Chiffonade Dressing
Apple Cobbler

MEAL NO. 3

Blanquette De Veau

Tiny Peas with Pearl Onions
Mashed Potatoes
Bibb Lettuce with French Dressing
Chocolate Mousse

Veal Del Mar

Because veal is a bit bland it is ideal to team with unusual ingredients, in this case, oysters.

3 pounds breast of veal
½ pint oysters with liquid
2 cups seasoned dry bread stuffing
¼ teaspoon salt

¼ teaspoon celery salt
⅛ teaspoon pepper
dash paprika
⅛ teaspoon basil

Heat oven to 350°F. Have the butcher prepare veal for stuffing, making a wide pocket. Drain oysters; reserve liquid. Chop oysters; combine with bread stuffing, oyster liquid, salts, pepper, paprika, and basil. Stuff pocket with mixture. Fasten opening with skewers. Place meat in a baking pan. Bake 1 hour or until tender. Makes 4 servings.

Pennsylvania Dutch Veal

3½ pounds breast of veal
2 tablespoons butter, softened
¾ teaspoon salt
¼ teaspoon celery salt
⅛ teaspoon pepper
¼ pound bulk pork sausage
¼ cup chopped onion
1 teaspoon grated orange rind

½ teaspoon lemon juice
⅛ teaspoon basil
⅛ teaspoon tarragon
6 tablespoons boiling water
1 cup seasoned dry bread stuffing
1 egg, slightly beaten
¾ cup chicken broth

Heat oven to 350°F. Have the butcher prepare veal for stuffing, making a wide pocket. Rub meat with butter, salts, and pepper. Sauté sausage; remove from skillet and drain. Sauté onion in sausage drippings until just tender. Combine orange rind, lemon juice, basil, tarragon, and boiling water; mix well. Pour mixture over bread stuffing. Add sausage, onion, and egg. Mix well and stuff pocket in the veal. Place in a baking pan and roast, uncovered, 1¼ hours or until tender. During last half hour of cooking, baste with broth. Serve meat with pan liquid, thickened if desired. Makes 4 servings.

Blanquette De Veau

There are many versions of this dish which are laborious and time-consuming—here's our shortcut version.

2 pounds breast of veal, cut into
3-inch cubes
12 small onions, peeled
2 cloves
1 carrot, diced
sprig of celery
4 sprigs of parsley

¾ teaspoon salt
pinch thyme
1 tablespoon flour
1 tablespoon water
2 egg yolks
2 tablespoons lemon juice
¼ teaspoon grated lemon rind

Put meat in a large kettle; add water to cover. Bring to a boil; reduce heat to simmer and skim. Add 2 of the onions stuck with cloves, carrot, celery, 1 sprig of the parsley, salt, and thyme. Simmer ¾ hour or until tender. Ten minutes before cooking time ends, add remaining onions. Strain broth. Put veal and onions on a heated platter. Make a paste of flour and water and stir into the broth until smooth. Add meat and onions. Beat egg yolks slightly with a little gravy; return to pan. Add lemon juice and lemon rind; stir. Heat 4 minutes. Do not boil. Garnish with remaining parsley and serve. Makes 4 servings.

BREAST OF VEAL—TWO

An unusual main dish with an interesting leftover bonus can be made from a breast of veal, which also yields a third dish to round out meals for three days. Have the butcher cut 1 pound of boned meat from a 6- to 7-pound breast of veal and have it ground. Ask him to cup a deep pocket in the breast for stuffing and to crack the bones in several places.

MEAL NO. 1

German Breast of Veal
with
Potato Stuffing

Buttered Brussels Sprouts
Mixed Raw Vegetable Salad with
Lemon and Oil Dressing
Apple Strudel

MEAL NO. 2

Ricardo's Veal and Kidney Beans

Buttered Zucchini
*Double Cornbread
Marinated Sliced Tomatoes
Spanish Flan

MEAL NO. 3

Creamed Veal Delon
with Noodles

Raw Spinach Salad
Honey Spice Cake

German Breast of Veal

The potato stuffing is a favorite with the Germans.

6-pound breast of veal	2 eggs
1 clove garlic, sliced	½ cup flour
3 teaspoons flour	1 teaspoon onion salt
½ teaspoon salt	⅛ teaspoon pepper
6 medium potatoes, pared	1 tablespoon minced parsley
1 onion, peeled	½ cup shortening, melted

Rub veal with garlic. Sprinkle with mixture of the 3 teaspoons flour and salt. Grate potatoes in a deep bowl; squeeze out excess moisture. Grate onion in the same bowl. Add eggs, the ½ cup flour, onion salt, pepper, and parsley. Mix well. Pour shortening over all and stir until well blended. Let stand 10 minutes. Heat oven to 325°F. Fill pocket of veal with this stuffing; fasten opening securely with skewers. Place meat in a baking pan; bake 3 to 3½ hours or until done. Makes 6 servings.

Ricardo's Veal and Kidney Beans

2 cups kidney beans	½ cup chopped parsley
10 cups water	1 clove garlic, minced
4 teaspoons salt	1 pound ground veal
3 teaspoons chili powder	2 tablespoons shortening
2 cups sliced onion	3 cups canned tomatoes, drained

Soak kidney beans in 6 cups of the water overnight. Drain; place in pan with remaining 4 cups of water, 2 teaspoons of the salt and 1½ teaspoons of the chili powder. Cover; bring to a boil. Reduce heat; simmer 3 hours. Drain; cool and store in refrigerator. Mix onion, parsley, and garlic; set aside. Brown meat in shortening in a large, heavy skillet. Add onion mixture and sauté 5 minutes. Add tomatoes and remaining salt and chili powder. Stir in the beans. Cover; simmer 20 to 25 minutes. Makes 6 servings.

Double Cornbread

1 cup flour	2 eggs, slightly beaten
1 cup yellow cornmeal	1 cup milk
4 teaspoons baking powder	3 tablespoons butter, melted
1 teaspoon salt	1 can (8¾ ounces) cream-style
¼ cup sugar	corn

Heat oven to 425°F. Grease a 9-inch square pan. Combine flour, cornmeal, baking powder, salt, and sugar; set aside. In a medium bowl, combine eggs, milk, butter, and corn. Add flour mixture, stirring only until flour mixture is moistened. Spoon batter into the prepared pan. Bake 25 to 30 minutes or until a knife inserted in the center comes out clean and top is golden brown. Cut into squares; serve hot. Makes 9 squares.

Creamed Veal Delon

4 tablespoons butter	1 cup diced cooked celery
¼ cup flour	1 cup cooked peas
1½ cups milk	2 tablespoons margarine
½ cup heavy cream	⅛ teaspoon thyme
1 teaspoon salt	¼ cup minced parsley
⅛ teaspoon white pepper	4 cups hot cooked noodles
2 cups diced cooked veal	4 sprigs parsley

Melt butter in a medium saucepan; blend in flour, stirring constantly. Gradually add milk and cook over low heat, stirring constantly, until sauce is thickened. Add cream and blend it in. Add salt and pepper. Cook 5 minutes, stirring frequently. Add veal, celery, and peas. Combine margarine, thyme and minced parsley. Add to hot noodles; mix well. Press noodles into an oiled 6-cup ring mold. Unmold on a hot serving plate; fill center with veal mixture. Garnish with parsley. Makes 6 servings.

LEG OF VEAL—ONE

A leg of veal can serve many a festive occasion and, if carefully planned from the beginning, it can yield a variety of delectable dishes. Order an 8-pound leg of veal; have butcher bone it and divide it into a 4-pound piece for roasting, a 2½-pound piece for the unusual veal-and-tuna dish, and a ¼ inch thick slice cut from the center part of the leg.

MEAL NO. 1

Roast Leg of Veal Mandarin

Baked Potatoes   Peas Amandine
Mixed Green Salad with Water Chestnuts and Capers
Orange Chiffon Pie

MEAL NO. 2

Vitello Tonnato

French Fried Potatoes
Julienne Carrots
Wilted Lettuce
Marble Cake with Chocolate Ice Cream

MEAL NO. 3

Wiener Schnitzel

Twice-baked potatoes   Buttered Zucchini
Cucumber and Tomato Salad
Linzer Torte

MEAL NO. 4

Veal Salad Flammarion

Potato Chips   Crisp Cauliflower
Mocha cake

Roast Leg of Veal Mandarin

Soy sauce lends a piquancy to veal and bacon adds extra flavor in this adaptation of an oriental delicacy.

4-pound leg of veal, boned
2 cloves garlic, cut in half
1 teaspoon salt
¼ teaspoon pepper

2 tablespoons soy sauce
6 slices bacon
½ teaspoon paprika

Heat oven to 325°F. Wipe meat with damp cloth. Rub it all over with cut garlic. Season with salt and pepper. Brush with soy sauce. Arrange bacon slices to cover top. Place veal in a baking pan. Sprinkle with paprika. Bake 2 to 2½ hours. Makes 8 servings.

Vitello Tonnato

A very popular Italian dish combining two unlikely ingredients—veal and tuna fish.

2½ pound piece of leg of veal, boned
1 small onion
2 cloves
1 small bay leaf
2 sprigs parsley
1 small stalk celery
⅛ teaspoon pepper

2 cans (6 ounces each) tuna fish
⅔ cup olive oil
2 teaspoons capers
8 chopped anchovies
⅛ teaspoon white pepper
½ cup lemon juice (approximately)
water cress

Place meat in a heavy kettle with water to cover. Add onion stuck with the cloves, bay leaf, parsley, celery, and pepper. Cover; simmer 1 hour or until tender. Remove meat. Cool and place on serving platter; slice. Combine tuna fish, olive oil, capers, anchovies, pepper, and enough lemon juice to taste. Work mixture until smooth using blender or mortar and pestle. Serve sauce with meat. Makes 6 servings.

Wiener Schnitzel

1½ pounds veal cut into 4 slices
  ¼ inch thick
1 teaspoon salt
¼ teaspoon pepper
1 egg, slightly beaten

¾ cup flour
¾ cup fine bread crumbs
½ cup butter
4 lemon slices
2 hard-cooked eggs, halved

Sprinkle veal slices with salt and pepper. Dip in egg, then in mixture of flour and bread crumbs. Let stand 25 minutes. Sauté slices in butter until tender and well browned on both sides. Serve with lemon slices and eggs. Makes 4 servings.

Veal Salad Flammarion

2 cups diced cooked veal
¼ cup chopped onion
¼ cup chopped celery
½ cup toasted blanched almonds
1 cup mayonnaise

1 teaspoon tarragon
1 tablespoon lemon juice
lettuce leaves
8 cherry tomatoes
8 ripe olives

Combine veal with onion, celery, and almonds. Mix mayonnaise with tarragon and lemon juice; blend well. Add enough mayonnaise mixture to veal mixture to bind it. Heap onto lettuce leaves. Garnish with tomatoes and olives and serve with extra mayonnaise mixture. Makes 4 servings.

LEG OF VEAL—TWO

A leg of veal will yield many interesting meals. Order an 8- to 9-pound leg and have butcher cut a 2-pound slice from the top of the leg. Have him pound this to ¼-inch thickness. Or place veal on a wooden board, remove the round center bone and pound meat with wooden mallet until thin enough to roll.

MEAL NO. 1

Lord Essex's Roast Leg of Veal

Wild and White Rice   French Artichokes
Romaine Salad with Lorenzo Dressing
Coffee Chiffon Pie

MEAL NO. 2

Veal and Ham Roll Beatrice

Baked Sweet Potatoes   Buttered Asparagus
Coleslaw
Cheesecake

MEAL NO. 3

Veal Braziliano

Scalloped Potatoes   Succotash
Mandarin Orange Salad
Spanish Cream   Macaroons

Lord Essex's Roast Leg of Veal

6- to 7-pound leg of veal,
  boned, rolled
4 veal kidneys, cleaned, rolled
  inside roast
½ cup butter
2 teaspoons salt
½ teaspoon pepper
¼ teaspoon thyme
¼ teaspoon sage
¼ teaspoon mace
¼ teaspoon rosemary

½ teaspoon basil
4 tender stalks celery, cut in half
3 medium carrots, sliced·
1 medium onion, sliced
2 shallots, chopped
½ cup white wine
1 cup beef bouillon
½ cup chicken bouillon
½ cup heavy cream
2 teaspoons tarragon
watercress

Heat oven to 350°F. Wipe meat with damp cloth. Combine half the butter with salt, pepper, and herbs. Spread mixture over meat. Melt remaining butter and pour into a baking pan, covering entire surface. Place meat in pan. Arrange vegetables around meat. Pour wine over all. Bake 2½ to 3 hours, basting frequently, or until tender. Remove meat to heated platter. Add bouillon to pan drippings, simmer 5 minutes. Strain into saucepan. Spoon off fat. Stir in cream and tarragon; heat through but do not boil. Serve in slices garnished with watercress. Makes 6 servings with leftovers.

Veal and Ham Roll Beatrice

2-pound slice of veal cut from
  top of leg
1 clove garlic, minced
2 teaspoons salt
1 medium onion, chopped
1 tablespoon butter
3 slices day old white bread,
  trimmed
1 pound ground lean raw ham

1 egg
¼ teaspoon pepper
½ teaspoon paprika
¼ teaspoon celery salt
⅛ teaspoon cayenne
2 tablespoons flour
2 tablespoons margarine, melted
¼ cup chopped green onions
1 cup water

Spread meat evenly with mixture of garlic and salt; set aside. Sauté onion in butter. Soak bread in cold water; squeeze dry. Mix with ham; add to onion. Combine egg, pepper, paprika, and celery salt. Beat slightly; knead into onion mixture; shape filling into an oblong roll. Place lengthwise in the center of the meat. Roll veal around filling; tie securely with string and secure with skewers. Heat oven to 325°F. Place veal roll in a baking pan. Combine cayenne and flour and sprinkle over meat. Pour melted margarine into pan; brown meat on all sides. Add green onions and blend in water. Place pan in oven; bake 1 to 1½ hours or until tender, basting frequently. When done, remove meat to heated platter; remove string and skewers, slice and serve with natural pan juices. Makes 6 servings.

Veal Braziliano

Olives, garlic, and chili powder combine to make this a zippy dish.

¾ cup butter	3 green stuffed olives, chopped
½ cup flour	½ clove garlic, minced
2 cups veal stock	2 hard-cooked eggs, coarsely
2 cups chicken broth	chopped
4 cups diced cooked veal	1¼ teaspoons chili powder
2 medium onions, minced	½ teaspoon salt
1 green pepper, chopped	¼ teaspoon pepper
¼ cup chopped pitted ripe olives	1½ cups soft bread crumbs

Heat oven to 350°F. Melt ½ cup of the butter in a medium skillet; blend in flour. Cook over low heat, stirring constantly, until mixture browns. Slowly add veal stock and chicken broth, stirring constantly until thickened. Add remaining ingredients, except bread crumbs. Pour mixture into a 2½-quart baking pan. Melt remaining ¼ cup butter; toss with bread crumbs. Top veal mixture with crumbs. Bake 30 to 35 minutes. Makes 4 servings.

RUMP OF VEAL—ONE

Order a 9-pound rump of veal and have the butcher bone it, reserving the bones. Have two pounds cut into very thin 2-inch strips. Have 1½ pounds cut into 6 pieces about ½ inch thick.

MEAL NO. 1

Poached Veal à la Vert

Creamed Carrots
Baked Potatoes
Tomatoes Vinaigrette
Apple Pie à la Mode

MEAL NO. 2

Finnish Hunter's Steak

Wild Rice with Toasted Almonds
Buttered Zucchini
Caesar Salad
Napoleons

MEAL NO. 3

Veal à la Française

French-Fried Potatoes
Buttered Green Beans
Molded Salad
Toffee Cake

Poached Veal à la Vert

A Parisian dish with a green sauce that's heavenly.

4 pounds rump of veal, boned
veal bones
2 teaspoons salt
1 teaspoon pepper
1 large clove garlic, minced
5 tablespoons finely chopped chives
5 tablespoons finely chopped
green pepper
3 tablespoons finely chopped
dill pickle
¼ cup capers, drained
5 tablespoons lemon juice
1 small clove garlic, minced
¼ cup vegetable oil
⅛ teaspoon sugar
2 dashes hot pepper sauce
1 dash Tabasco

Place meat and bones in a medium kettle; cover with water. Add salt, pepper, and large clove garlic. Bring to boiling, reduce heat, cover, and simmer 2 to 2½ hours or until meat is fork tender, turning meat occasionally. Combine chives, green pepper, pickle, capers, lemon juice, small clove garlic, vegetable oil, sugar, hot pepper sauce and Tabasco in a small saucepan. Add 1 cup of the veal broth. Heat slowly to boiling point, stirring occasionally. Turn meat onto a hot platter; slice. Spoon over some of the sauce and serve the rest in a separate bowl. Makes 6 servings.

Finnish Hunter's Steak

2 pounds veal cut into very thin 2-inch strips	½ pound fresh mushrooms, sliced
4 tablespoons flour	1 medium onion, sliced
¾ teaspoon salt	½ teaspoon onion salt
¼ teaspoon pepper	⅛ teaspoon white pepper
⅛ teaspoon paprika	1½ cups milk
6 tablespoons butter	½ cup light cream

Roll meat in a mixture of 2 tablespoons of the flour, salt, pepper, and paprika. Melt 2 tablespoons of the butter in a large, heavy skillet; add meat and brown all over. Remove meat from pan; keep hot. Add remaining butter to skillet. Add mushrooms and onion. Cook, stirring, 5 minutes. Stir in remaining flour, onion salt, and white pepper. Blend in milk and cream, stirring constantly over medium heat until smooth and thickened. Pour sauce over veal on a hot platter and serve. Makes 6 servings.

Veal à la Française

1½ pounds veal, cut into 6 pieces	1 clove garlic, minced
6 tablespoons flour	1 cup consommé
¾ teaspoon salt	½ cup chicken broth
¼ teaspoon pepper	2 cups canned tomatoes, drained, sliced
½ cup bacon drippings	1 cup canned mushrooms
1 small onion, chopped	
1 tablespoon chopped parsley	

Heat oven to 350°F. Dredge veal in a mixture of 2 tablespoons of the flour, salt, and pepper. Heat bacon drippings in a large, heavy skillet; add onion, parsley, and garlic; cook until golden brown. Remove from fat. Brown meat in the skillet; remove to a platter. Add remaining flour to skillet. Stir until browned. Add consommé and chicken broth. Cook, stirring constantly, until smooth. Arrange tomatoes in a 1½-quart baking dish. Place meat on top. Pour sauce over it. Cover; bake 45 to 50 minutes. During last 15 minutes of cooking add mushrooms and continue baking uncovered. Makes 6 servings.

RUMP OF VEAL—TWO

A 7-pound veal rump makes delicious meals in many ways. Veal is the main meat of Germany, Switzerland and Italy and, being white meat, it should be cooked slowly and thoroughly. Have a rump of veal boned and cut into a 4-pound and a 3-pound piece. Save the bones.

MEAL NO. 1

Veal with Anchovy Paste Marceline

Asparagus with Hollandaise Sauce
Whipped Potatoes
Tomato Aspic with Artichoke Hearts
Fruit with Assorted Cheeses

MEAL NO. 2

Veal Anastasia

Stuffed Potatoes   Harvard Beets
Cold Green Beans with French Dressing
Ice Cream and Florentines

MEAL NO. 3

Party Jellied Veal Loaf

Corn Soufflé   Pink Potato Salad
Avocado on the Half Shell
Cream-Frosted Chocolate Mousse

Veal with Anchovy Paste Marceline

In Brussels I had a taste of this extraordinary concoction and cornered the chef for the recipe.

veal bones
1 quart water
½ teaspoon salt
2 peppercorns
¼ teaspoon dry mustard
1½ tablespoons anchovy paste
1½ teaspoons lemon juice

1½ cloves garlic, minced
¼ teaspoon pepper
2 teaspoons grated lemon rind
3 to 4 pounds veal rump, boned
5 slices bacon
1 tablespoon flour

Put bones, water, salt, and peppercorns in a large, heavy kettle; cover and simmer 4 hours. Strain and reserve stock. Cool and then remove fat. Combine mustard with anchovy paste, lemon juice, garlic, pepper, and lemon rind; mix well. Spread ⅓ of paste inside meat. Roll up tight and secure with string. Spread remaining paste all over outside of veal. Cover lightly with foil; let stand at room temperature 1½ hours.

Heat oven to 350°F. Place meat in a baking pan; cover top with bacon slices. Bake, uncovered, 2 to 2½ hours. Remove bacon 15 minutes before end of baking time. Turn meat onto a heated platter. Remove fat from liquid in baking pan. Add 1½ cups reserved veal stock. Stir well. Heat to simmering. Thicken slightly with flour. Cook, stirring, until smooth. Makes 6 servings.

Veal Anastasia

3 pounds veal rump, boned
1 teaspoon salt
½ pound fresh mushrooms, halved
½ cup chopped celery
½ cup chopped onion
¼ cup butter
2 tablespoons flour

2 tablespoons water
¾ teaspoon salt
⅛ teaspoon pepper
¾ cup commercial sour cream
6 bacon slices, crisply cooked,
    crumbled

Place meat in a deep, heavy kettle; cover with cold water. Add salt. Cover; simmer 2 hours or until tender. Remove meat; cool slightly. Reserve stock. Cut meat into 1½-inch cubes. Sauté mushrooms, celery, and onion in butter until lightly browned. Heat oven to 375°F. Make a smooth paste of flour and water; add to 2 cups of veal stock. Season with salt and pepper. Cook, stirring constantly, until thickened. Place meat and vegetables in a 1½-quart baking dish. Pour gravy over all. Bake 15 minutes. Cover top with sour cream. Sprinkle with crumbled bacon; serve immediately. Makes 6 servings.

Party Jellied Veal Loaf

An inexpensive but delicious way to serve a crowd.

3 cups ground cooked veal
2 tablespoons minced onion
¾ cup finely diced cucumber
¼ cup diced celery
2 tablespoons cold water

1 tablespoon (1 envelope) unflavored gelatin
1¾ cups medium white sauce, hot
1 cup chilled evaporated milk

Combine veal, onion, cucumber, and celery; set aside. Soak gelatin in water. Add to hot white sauce; stir until dissolved. Add veal mixture to sauce. Chill. When veal mixture begins to set, whip evaporated milk stiff and fold in quickly and thoroughly. Pour into an 8-cup mold. Refrigerate overnight or until set. Turn out on a serving platter and slice when ready to serve. Makes 12 servings.

SHOULDER OF VEAL—ONE

Have the butcher bone a 7-pound shoulder of veal, dividing it thus: one 3-pound piece cut open and laid flat; 2 pounds cut for stew; and 2 pounds cut into 1-½ inch cubes. Save the bones.

MEAL NO. 1

Veal Roll Allemande

Scalloped Potatoes   Buttered Lima Beans
*Coleslaw with Grapes
Spiced Fruit Compote

MEAL NO. 2

Gettysburg Veal

Stewed Tomatoes with Croutons
Corn Soufflé
Mixed Green Salad
Lady Baltimore Cake

MEAL NO. 3

Veal à la Russe

Pilaf   Lemon-Glazed Carrots
Cucumber and Tomato Salad
Date Nut Torte

Veal Roll Allemande

A German hausfrau served me this while I was traveling through Germany one fall, and she kindly gave me the recipe.

1 medium onion, finely chopped	⅛ teaspoon oregano
¾ cup finely chopped mushrooms	⅛ teaspoon basil
1 tablespoon butter	⅛ teaspoon pepper
1 cup sauerkraut and liquid	1 egg, slightly beaten
1 cup dry bread crumbs	3 pounds shoulder of veal, boned
1 tablespoon chopped parsley	2 cans (10½ ounces each)
1 teaspoon chopped celery	consommé
½ teaspoon salt	1 tablespoon flour
⅛ teaspoon rosemary	½ cup water
⅛ teaspoon thyme	⅛ teaspoon paprika

Heat oven to 325°F. Sauté onion and mushrooms in butter in a heavy skillet 10 minutes or until butter is absorbed, stirring constantly so that vegetables will not brown. Drain and reserve liquid from sauerkraut. Combine bread crumbs, sauerkraut, onion and mushroom mixture, parsley, celery, salt, herbs, pepper, and egg; mix well. Lay meat open and spread with stuffing, leaving ½ inch uncovered on all sides. Roll up jelly-roll fashion; tie with string and secure with skewers. Place in a baking pan. Combine sauerkraut juice with 1 can of the consommé; pour over veal. Bake, uncovered, 2½ to 3 hours or until fork tender, basting occasionally. Remove meat to a heated platter. Add remaining can of consommé and water to pan drippings. Bring to a boil. Thicken with a paste made of flour and water. Sprinkle with paprika. Cook and stir until well blended. Makes 4 servings.

Coleslaw with Grapes

4 cups shredded white cabbage	1 cup seedless green grapes
¾ cup Sour Cream Dressing	

Mix cabbage and dressing thoroughly. Add grapes and toss carefully with a fork. Makes 4 servings.

Sour Cream Dressing

1 cup commercial sour cream
2 tablespoons sugar
½ teaspoon dry mustard
½ teaspoon paprika
1 teaspoon salt
3 tablespoons vinegar
1 egg

Combine all ingredients; heat in top of double boiler 3 minutes or until dressing thickens, stirring constantly. Cool to room temperature; store in refrigerator. Makes 1½ cups.

Gettysburg Veal

1 teaspoon salt
¼ teaspoon celery salt
⅛ teaspoon pepper
¼ teaspoon nutmeg
¼ teaspoon mace
¼ teaspoon dry mustard
¼ cup flour
2 pounds shoulder of veal, boned,
    cut for stew
3 tablespoons shortening
1¼ cups orange juice
¼ cup lemon juice
3 tablespoons grated orange rind
1 small clove garlic, crushed
1 tablespoon vinegar
2 cups water
¾ cup seedless raisins
¼ cup chopped almonds

Combine salts, pepper, nutmeg, mace, dry mustard, and flour. Heat shortening in a medium skillet. Roll pieces of meat in seasoned flour; reserve remaining flour mixture to thicken gravy. Brown meat well. Add orange and lemon juices, orange rind, garlic, and vinegar; cover and simmer 45 minutes or until meat is tender. Add water and thicken with remaining seasoned flour. Add raisins and almonds; simmer 10 minutes. Makes 4 servings.

Veal à la Russe

2 pounds veal shoulder, boned, cut
    into 1½-inch cubes
veal bones
1½ teaspoons salt
½ pound mushrooms
4 tablespoons butter
¼ cup chopped celery
¼ cup chopped parsley
½ cup chopped onion
2 tablespoons flour
dash cayenne
¾ cup commercial sour cream
8 slices bacon, cooked crisp and
    crumbled

Place meat in a large, heavy skillet, with bones. Cover with cold water and 1 teaspoon of the salt. Cover; simmer 2 hours or until tender. Remove bones; skim off foam. Strain and reserve broth. Cut mushrooms in half; sauté in butter with celery, parsley, and onion until light brown. Set aside. Mix flour with a little water to make a paste. Add to 2 cups reserved veal broth; add remaining salt and cayenne. Cook, stirring, until thickened. Heat oven to 375°F. Place meat and vegetables in a 2-quart baking dish. Pour gravy over all. Bake 20 minutes. Add sour cream. Sprinkle with bacon and serve immediately. Makes 4 servings.

SHOULDER OF VEAL—TWO

Order a 7-pound shoulder of veal and have the butcher bone it. For the following three meals you will need a 3½-pound piece, rolled and tied, 2 pounds cut into 1½-inch cubes, and 1½ pounds ground. Save the bones.

MEAL NO. 1

Jaipur Veal Curry

Corn Fritters   Okra and Tomatoes
Citrus Fruit Salad with French Dressing
Lemon Chiffon Pie

MEAL NO. 1

Veal Di Brangata

*Fluffy Risotto   Buttered Asparagus
Hearts of Lettuce with Herbed Dressing
Pear Zabaglione

MEAL NO. 3

Veal Patties with Mushrooms

Julienne Potatoes
Wax Beans au Gratin
Tray of Crisped Greens
Fruit Compote   Cookies

Jaipur Veal Curry

¼ teaspoon marjoram
¼ teaspoon thyme
⅛ teaspoon sage
2 teaspoons curry powder
¾ teaspoon salt
¼ teaspoon onion salt
⅛ teaspoon pepper
⅛ teaspoon paprika
3½ pounds shoulder of veal,
  boned and rolled

3 tablespoons vegetable oil
3 tablespoons flour
1½ cups canned chicken broth
½ cup consommé
2 small cloves garlic, minced
2 medium onions, chopped
veal bones
1 large apple, with skin, cored,
  quartered
¼ cup currants

Combine marjoram, thyme, sage, curry powder, salts, pepper, and paprika; mix well. Brush meat over entire surface with 1 tablespoon vegetable oil. Rub in mixed seasonings. Dredge veal with 1½ tablespoons of the flour, rubbing it in well. Pour remaining vegetable oil into a large kettle; brown meat evenly on all sides. Pour in 1 cup of the chicken broth and the consommé. Add garlic, onions, veal bones, apple, and currants. Reduce heat; cover kettle tightly and simmer 1½ hours or until fork tender, turning meat frequently. Remove meat to a heated platter and keep warm. If tied, remove strings. Remove bones from liquid and pour off excess fat. Combine remaining flour and chicken broth, blending until smooth. Add to kettle and cook, stirring, until thickened. Strain gravy; serve separately. Makes six servings.

Veal Di Brangata

An Italian friend of mine and I developed this recipe.

2 pounds veal shoulder, cut into
  1½-inch cubes
1½ tablespoons flour
¼ teaspoon pepper
3 tablespoons olive oil
1 clove garlic, crushed
1 large onion, thinly sliced
½ teaspoon rosemary
¼ teaspoon basil

¼ teaspoon celery seed
1 teaspoon salt
¼ cup tomato sauce
½ cup chicken broth
½ cup white wine
16 pitted ripe olives, sliced
½ cup minced parsley
1 tablespoon minced celery

Remove fat or gristle from veal cubes if there is any. Combine flour with pepper and dredge meat well. Pour olive oil in a large skillet; brown meat well. Add garlic and onion. Sauté until onion is transparent, about 5 minutes. Add rosemary, basil, celery seed, salt, tomato sauce, chicken broth, and wine. Cover; simmer 2 hours or until tender. If necessary, add a little boiling water. At the end of the first hour add olives. Add parsley and celery 20 minutes before meat is done. Serve hot. Makes six servings.

Fluffy Risotto

1 cup rice
¼ cup butter
4 cups chicken broth, hot
½ cup grated Cheddar cheese
⅛ teaspoon cayenne
¼ teaspoon paprika
⅛ teaspoon saffron
2 teaspoons salt
1 large clove garlic, minced

Sauté rice in butter in a medium skillet until straw-colored, stirring frequently. Pour hot broth over rice. Add cheese, cayenne, paprika, saffron, salt, and garlic; blend well. Transfer mixture to top of double boiler; steam over hot water 55 minutes. Makes six servings.

Veal Patties with Mushrooms

A many-flavored dish fit for a king and adapted to our tastes.

1½ pounds ground veal
⅓ cup finely chopped celery
¼ cup minced parsley
1 tablespoon finely chopped raw carrot
1 cup soft bread crumbs
⅓ cup milk
⅓ cup light cream
2 eggs, slightly beaten
¾ tablespoon grated onion
1½ teaspoons salt
⅛ teaspoon pepper
⅛ teaspoon paprika
pinch thyme
pinch marjoram
pinch basil
¼ cup shortening
⅔ cup water
1 can (10½ ounces) cream of mushroom soup
½ cup canned mushrooms, coarsely chopped
1 teaspoon Worcestershire sauce

Combine veal, celery, parsley, carrot, bread crumbs, milk, cream, eggs, onion, salt, pepper, paprika, thyme, marjoram, and basil. Mix all together thoroughly. Shape into 18 patties, handling them carefully as mixture will be soft. Brown patties, a few at a time, in shortening in a skillet. Heat oven to 350°F. Place patties in a shallow baking pan. Drain off excess fat and add water to drippings in skillet. Stir and cook 5 minutes over medium heat. Blend in mushroom soup and mushrooms. Stir in Worcestershire sauce. Pour over patties. Bake 30 minutes, basting patties occasionally. Makes six servings.

CHICKEN

ROAST CHICKEN—ONE

A delicately scented roast chicken for the main meal, an unusual Mexican Chicken Pie, and Haitian Chicken Turnovers are the rewards for careful planning.

MEAL NO. 1

Roast Chicken Oreganaki

Corn Soufflé   Buttered Artichoke Hearts
Cinnamon Pear Halves
Carrot and Celery Sticks
Orange Chiffon Pie

MEAL NO. 2

Mexican Chicken Pie

Buttered Garbanzos   Stewed Tomatoes
Green Salad
Honey Cake

MEAL NO. 3

Haitian Chicken Turnovers

Green Peas with Mushrooms
Buttered Beets
Lettuce Wedges with Caesar Dressing
Lemon Icebox Dessert

Roast Chicken Oreganaki

5- to 6-pound roasting chicken
½ cup butter
¼ cup lemon juice
¾ cup dry white wine
1 teaspoon salt
⅛ teaspoon pepper
1 teaspoon oregano
¼ teaspoon thyme
1 clove garlic
½ cup boiling water

Heat oven to 325°F. Wipe chicken with damp cloth. In a small saucepan, melt butter and add lemon juice, 2 tablespoons of the wine, salt, pepper, oregano, and thyme. Brush chicken with mixture inside and out. Place garlic inside chicken. Place chicken in a roasting pan; combine remaining butter sauce with remaining wine and boiling water and pour over chicken. Cover chicken with aluminum foil and bake 45 minutes. Remove foil, baste chicken, and cover again with foil. Baste in this manner every 25 minutes for 2½ hours or until chicken is tender. Skim fat from drippings. Serve sauce with chicken. Makes 4 servings with leftovers.

Mexican Chicken Pie

One-plate meal designed to be consumed quickly and with pleasure.

2 cups water
1½ teaspoons salt
½ cup corn meal
2 sweetbreads
3 tablespoons flour
2 cups coarsely diced cooked chicken
5 tablespoons butter
½ teaspoon chopped parsley

3 canned artichoke bottoms, drained and quartered
½ teaspoon chopped celery
1½ cups light cream
½ cup heavy cream
¼ cup sherry
½ teaspoon salt
¼ teaspoon pepper

Bring water to a rapid boil; add salt. Reduce heat; very slowly add corn meal in a thin stream, stirring constantly and rapidly as it thickens. Place in top of double boiler over hot water and cook, uncovered, 30 minutes. Spread on a well-greased pan to ½-inch thickness. Chill overnight.

Put sweetbreads in cold water; let stand 1 hour; drain. Cover with boiling water, adding 1 teaspoon salt and 2 tablespoons lemon juice. Simmer 20 minutes, drain, and plunge into cold water. When sweetbreads are cold, remove membranes and tubes; dice. Put flour in a paper bag and shake sweetbread pieces in it. Sprinkle remaining flour over chicken. Melt 3 tablespoons of the butter in a heavy skillet; add chicken and sweetbreads and lightly brown. Heat oven to 400°F. Turn chicken and sweetbreads into a 2-quart baking dish. Add artichoke bottoms. Sprinkle with parsley and celery. Pour creams in the skillet in which meats were browned; cook 5 minutes, stirring constantly. Add sherry; pour cream sauce over meats. Spread with cold corn meal mush and remaining butter. Bake 20 minutes. Makes 4 servings.

Haitian Chicken Turnovers

The island's contribution to Monday's leftover.

¼ pound unsalted butter
¼ pound mushrooms, thinly sliced
2 cups diced cooked chicken
1½ cups heavy cream
½ cup light cream
1 tablespoon sherry
2 tablespoons dry white wine
½ teaspoon salt

⅛ teaspoon pepper
2 tablespoons flour
2 tablespoons butter
2 cups hot cooked spaghettini
3 tablespoons grated Parmesan cheese
½ teaspoon basil

Heat oven to 375°F. Melt ¼ pound unsalted butter in a large, heavy skillet; add mushrooms and sauté 3 minutes. Add chicken, creams, wines, salt, and pepper; heat almost to boiling. Combine flour and the 2 tablespoons butter to make a smooth paste; stir into chicken mixture and continue cooking over low heat, stirring constantly until thickened. Spread spaghettini in bottom of a shallow, greased 1½-quart baking dish. Pour chicken mixture over it. Sprinkle with cheese and basil. Bake 20 minutes or until top is golden brown. Makes 4 servings.

ROAST CHICKEN—TWO

Poultry meals can be made exciting by varying the stuffings. Even a 4-pound roasting chicken can yield two leftover meals for the smaller family and here is our version.

MEAL NO. 1

Roast Chicken
with Pilgrim Bread Stuffing

Glazed Sweet Potatoes with Marshmallows
Creamed Onions   Buttered Peas
Bibb Lettuce with White French Dressing
Swiss Chocolate Cake

MEAL NO. 2

Chicken à la Russe

Creamed Corn　　　Baked Zucchini
Beet Salad
Butterscotch Pie

MEAL NO. 3

Golden Chicken Soufflé

Parslied Potatoes　　　Peas and Onions
Orange and Grapefruit Salad
Spumoni Ice Cream

Roast Chicken
with Pilgrim Bread Stuffing

4-pound ready-to-cook chicken
1 recipe Pilgrim Bread Stuffing
 (see below)

2 teaspoons butter, melted
1 teaspoon lemon juice

Stuff the chicken and truss it. Heat oven to 325°F. Place chicken on rack of roasting pan. Brush with a mixture of the butter and lemon juice. Bake 1½ to 2 hours or until done. Makes 4 servings with leftovers.

Pilgrim Bread Stuffing

Use 1 cup of stuffing for each pound of the ready-to-cook weight. The recipe below is for a 4-pound chicken.

⅓ cup butter
¼ cup finely minced onion
4 cups coarse, dry bread crumbs
 or bread cubes
¼ cup chopped celery
¼ cup chopped parsley
1 tablespoon chopped walnut meats
1 teaspoon salt

¼ teaspoon pepper
½ teaspoon dried sage
¼ teaspoon thyme
¼ teaspoon marjoram
poultry seasoning to taste
 (½ to 1 teaspoon)
hot chicken broth

Melt butter in a large, heavy skillet. Add onion and cook until yellow, stirring occasionally. Stir in 1 cup of the bread crumbs. Heat, stirring to prevent excessive browning. Turn into a deep bowl. Mix in remaining ingredients lightly. For dry stuffing, add little or no broth. For a moist stuffing, mix in lightly with a fork just enough hot broth to moisten the dry crumbs. Cool; place stuffing loosely in chicken when ready to bake. Makes 1 quart.

Chicken à la Russe

1 tablespoon butter	¼ cup chopped, sautéed
2 teaspoons flour	mushrooms
½ cup light cream	pancake batter (to make 8
½ teaspoon salt	pancakes)
⅛ teaspoon pepper	½ cup commercial sour cream
1 cup chopped cooked chicken	¼ cup grated Cheddar cheese
¼ cup chopped almonds	2 tablespoons butter

Heat oven to 375°F. Melt butter in a medium skillet; blend in flour. Cook 1 minute. Add cream gradually, stirring constantly, until sauce is smooth and thick. Season with salt and pepper; simmer over low heat 1 minute. Add chicken, almonds, and mushrooms; mix well. Use your favorite pancake batter. Make 8 large, thin pancakes. As each is done, top with a generous tablespoonful of chicken mixture, roll up, and arrange side by side in a greased, shallow 2-quart baking dish. Place 1 teaspoon sour cream on top of each roll. Sprinkle with cheese and dot with butter. Bake 20 minutes. Makes 4 servings.

Golden Chicken Soufflé

3 tablespoons butter	⅛ teaspoon pepper
3 tablespoons flour	1 cup coarsely chopped cooked
¼ cup milk	chicken
¼ cup light cream	1 teaspoon minced parsley
½ cup condensed cream of	1 teaspoon finely cut chives
mushroom soup	dash paprika
½ teaspoon salt	3 eggs, separated

Heat oven to 350°F. Melt butter in a medium skillet; stir in flour and cook 1 minute. Gradually add milk and cream, stirring constantly. Add soup; continue stirring until smooth and thick. Season with salt and pepper and simmer 3 to 4 minutes. Add chicken, parsley, chives, paprika, and well-beaten egg yolks, stirring constantly. Cool to lukewarm. Beat egg whites until stiff but not dry; fold in gently. Turn into a greased 1-quart casserole. Bake 35 to 45 minutes or until soufflé is firm. Makes 4 servings.

ROAST CHICKEN—THREE

Two 5-pound roasting chickens can give you four excellent meals, each one "gourmet" enough for company. Serve the roast chickens with Napoleon's Brandy Sauce for a gala occasion. Plan a luncheon for your bridge party and two more meals which no one will guess were made with leftovers.

MEAL NO. 1

Roast Chicken with Pecan Stuffing

*Napoleon's Brandy Sauce
Whipped Parslied Potatoes
Peas and Onions
Cheese   Apples
Irish Coffee

MEAL NO. 2

Japanese Chicken Mousse

Boiled Baby Carrots   Sesame Toast
Petits Fours

MEAL NO. 3

Southern Lady Casserole

Buttered Broccoli
Cranberry Jelly
Mocha Cake

MEAL NO. 4

Poulet en Crème

Hot Cornbread   Buttered Peas
Tossed Green Salad
Raspberry Turnovers

Roast Chicken with Pecan Stuffing

2 5-pound roasting chickens
6 tablespoons butter
3 medium onions, chopped
3 celery stalks, chopped
½ teaspoon basil
½ teaspoon thyme
½ teaspoon sage
1½ teaspoons salt

½ teaspoon paprika
7 cups soft white bread crumbs
1½ teaspoons minced parsley
½ cup chopped almonds
1 cup chopped pecans
Napoleon's Brandy Sauce (see
  below)

Wipe chickens with a damp cloth. To make the stuffing, melt butter in a large skillet. Add onions and celery and sauté until tender. Add seasonings and stir. Mix bread crumbs, parsley, and nuts in a large bowl. Add onion and celery mixture and blend well. Stuff chickens and truss them. Heat oven to 300°F. Place chickens in an open pan and roast 2 to 2½ hours until tender and brown. Transfer chickens to a serving platter. Reserve pan drippings.

Napoleon's Brandy Sauce

½ cup butter
½ cup flour
4 cups milk, scalded
¾ teaspoon salt

1 cup heavy cream
½ cup brandy
pan drippings from roast chicken

Melt butter in a saucepan; add flour and beat with a rotary beater over medium heat for 4 minutes. Add milk and salt. Stir and bring to a boil; reduce heat, simmer 1 minute. Add cream and brandy. Remove fat from roasting pan drippings. Add cream sauce to pan; blend well and heat through. Strain and serve piping hot in a gravy boat.

Japanese Chicken Mousse

A westernized Japanese delicacy for a special occasion.

3 egg yolks, slightly beaten
⅛ teaspoon onion salt
⅛ teaspoon salt
¼ teaspoon celery salt
¼ teaspoon paprika
1 cup hot chicken broth
1 envelope unflavored gelatin
¼ cup cold water

¾ cup minced cooked chicken
¼ cup chopped toasted almonds
¼ cup chopped filberts
½ cup seedless white grapes
½ teaspoon grated onion
1 cup heavy cream, whipped
4 tablespoons saké or sherry

Combine egg yolks, salts, and paprika in top of a double boiler. Gradually pour hot broth over mixture; cook over hot water until thickened, stirring constantly. Soften gelatin in water and add to mixture, stirring until dissolved. Remove from heat; add chicken, nuts, grapes, and onion. Cool to lukewarm; fold in whipped cream and wine. Pour into a 4-cup mold. Chill until firm. Unmold on a chilled platter. Serve with mayonnaise. Makes 6 servings.

Southern Lady Casserole

2 cups chicken broth
2 cups cooked rice
¼ cup butter
¼ cup flour
1½ cups milk
½ cup light cream
½ teaspoon salt
⅛ teaspoon pepper
1 tablespoon minced onion
⅛ teaspoon ground ginger
¼ teaspoon nutmeg

pinch mace
3 cups diced cooked chicken
1½ cups sliced mushrooms, sautéed slightly
½ cup chopped walnuts
¼ cup blanched almonds, toasted, chopped
2 cups fresh bread crumbs, buttered
½ teaspoon paprika

Heat oven to 300°F. Pour half the chicken broth over rice and stir well; set aside. Melt butter in a large, heavy skillet; blend in flour and cook 1 minute. Stir in remaining chicken broth, milk, and cream. Stir until smooth; simmer until thickened. Add seasonings, onion and spices. In a greased 2-quart baking dish arrange layers of rice, chicken, cream sauce, mushrooms, and nuts; repeat until all is used. Sprinkle crumbs on top; sprinkle with paprika. Bake 35 minutes or until browned. Makes 6 servings.

Poulet en Crème

So quick to prepare—perfect for busy days.

3 cups cooked chicken, diced
3 cups heavy cream, scalded
2 egg yolks, well beaten

½ cup sherry, warmed
½ teaspoon salt
dash white pepper

Add chicken to scalded cream. Add a little of this to beaten egg yolks, then stir yolks into cream mixture. Bring almost to a boil. Stir in wine; season with salt and pepper. Makes 6 servings.

FRYING CHICKENS

For a truly different planned-over array of meals, buy three frying chickens, 2½ to 3 pounds each. Have the butcher bone the breasts, leaving them whole; separate thighs from drumsticks and use remaining parts (wings, backs, and bones) for broth and a light meal.

MEAL NO. 1

Deviled Drumsticks

Home-fried Potatoes   Wax Beans and Onion Rings
Creamy Cabbage Slaw
Pineapple Upside-down Cake

MEAL NO. 2

Chicken Breasts Eugénie

New Potatoes   Fresh Asparagus
Mixed Green Salad
Melon and Prosciutto

MEAL NO. 3

Chicken Almond and Eggs Blanchard

Canadian Bacon   Shoestring Potatoes
Orange and Avocado Salad
Pound Cake

MEAL NO. 4

Chicken Thighs with Walnut Sauce

Buttered Rice   Brussels Sprouts
Lima Bean Salad
Pecan Pie

Deviled Drumsticks

A Continental favorite served hot or cold.

6 chicken drumsticks
1 small carrot, diced
1 small onion, sliced
pinch marjoram
½ teaspoon salt

⅛ teaspoon pepper
½ cup prepared mustard
½ cup butter, melted
dash Tabasco

Cook drumsticks in water with carrot, onion, and marjoram 12 minutes or until just tender. Drain. Score skin lightly. Combine remaining ingredients. Generously coat drumsticks with mixture. Refrigerate overnight. Just before serving, broil drumsticks 3 inches from source of heat about 15 minutes, turning frequently and brushing with sauce. Remove to a heated platter. Heat remaining sauce, pour over drumsticks, and serve. Makes 4 servings.

Chicken Breasts Eugénie

Chicken and ham superbly complement one another in this haute cuisine company dish.

3 boned chicken breasts
3 tablespoons butter
4 slices cooked ham, ¼ inch thick
3 tablespoons flour
1 cup heavy cream
1 cup light cream
¾ teaspoon salt

¼ teaspoon white pepper
3 egg yolks
½ cup Madeira
8 large mushroom caps
2 tablespoons butter, melted
4 slices toast
4 sprigs parsley

Heat oven to 350°F. Sauté chicken in butter in a large, heavy skillet until golden. Remove from skillet and keep warm. Fry ham in same butter, turning over once, until browned; remove and keep warm. Stir in flour to make a paste. Slowly add creams, stirring constantly until well blended. Season with salt and pepper. Beat egg yolks and slowly add some of cream mixture; add yolks to cream sauce and stir until well blended. Strain. Clean skillet and return sauce to it. Add chicken and ham; simmer very gently 15 minutes, stirring occasionally. Do not boil. Add Madeira. Sauté mushrooms in melted butter in a small skillet. To serve place 1 slice of toast in each of 4 heatproof individual casseroles. Lay a slice of ham and a portion of chicken breast in each. Place two mushroom caps on top of each. Pour sauce over. Cover and bake 10 minutes or until heated. Serve at once. Garnish with parsley. Makes 4 servings.

Chicken Almond and Eggs Blanchard

I adapted the French Provençale dish by borrowing from a Chinese method of cooking chicken and thus combined East and West.

leftover chicken parts
4 tablespoons butter
½ cup blanched, toasted almonds, finely chopped
1 small onion, minced
dash Tabasco
dash Worcestershire sauce

¼ teaspoon chili powder
¼ teaspoon curry powder
½ cup light cream
¼ cup dry white wine
4 eggs, lightly beaten
½ teaspoon salt
⅛ teaspoon pepper

Barely cover chicken parts with lightly salted water and boil until meat falls from bones. Discard skin and bones and shred enough meat to make 1 cup finely chopped chicken. Boil broth down to ¼ cup; set aside. Melt butter in a heavy skillet; add almonds, onion, seasonings and chicken. Brown lightly, stirring frequently. Stir in cream, reserved broth, and wine. Cook until liquid has almost evaporated. Pour in eggs; season with salt and pepper. Stir gently until just set. Serve at once. Makes 4 servings.

Chicken Thighs with Walnut Sauce

6 chicken thighs
½ teaspoon salt
⅛ teaspoon pepper
¼ cup flour
¼ cup butter
1 small onion, finely chopped
⅓ cup dry white wine

1 cup boiling water
2 tablespoons cornstarch
½ cup milk
½ cup light cream
2 egg yolks
½ cup finely ground walnuts
2 tablespoons chopped parsley

Sprinkle chicken thighs with salt and pepper; dredge with flour. Melt butter in a heavy skillet. Add onion and chicken and brown on all sides. Add wine, cover, and simmer 10 minutes. Add boiling water, cover, and cook over low heat 45 minutes. Remove chicken to a pan; keep warm. Combine cornstarch, milk, and cream. Slowly add mixture to stock in skillet, stirring constantly. Beat egg yolks slightly. Add some of hot sauce to egg yolks, pour all into the skillet, stirring over low heat until thickened. Add walnuts and cook 5 minutes longer. Return chicken thighs to sauce; heat through for a few minutes. Makes 4 servings.

STEWING CHICKEN

Even a large stewing chicken can yield some very tempting second and third meals which look and taste as if they had been planned individually as gourmet treats.

MEAL NO. 1

Chicken Salad Romeo

Cream Cheese and Date Nut Bread Sandwiches
Shoestring Potatoes
Crème St. Honoré

MEAL NO. 2

Chicken Pickle Aspic Dryone

Open Face Danish Sandwiches
German Potato Salad
Sliced Peaches in White Wine
Cookies

MEAL NO. 3

Tomato Soup

Chicken Turnovers Alex

Buttered Asparagus   Pickled Beets
Apricot Whip with Madeira

Chicken Salad Romeo

7-pound stewing chicken
3 small onions
2 stalks celery
1 bay leaf
1 teaspoon salt
leftover veal stock or chicken
    bouillon
¼ cup heavy cream, whipped
¼ cup mayonnaise

1½ teaspoons ketchup
½ teaspoon Worcestershire sauce
½ teaspoon Tabasco
2 tablespoons lemon juice
¼ teaspoon cognac
1 large orange, peeled, sectioned
1 firm banana, sliced
1¼ cups seedless green grapes

Simmer chicken, onions, celery, bay leaf, and salt in veal stock or bouillon for 3 hours. Remove chicken. Pull off skin, bone, and return skin and bones to stock. Simmer 2 hours. Cool and refrigerate stock. Reserve for other recipe. Cool chicken meat. Cube half of it into 1½-inch cubes; refrigerate. Reserve remaining meat for other recipe. Combine whipped cream, mayonnaise, ketchup, Worcestershire sauce, Tabasco, lemon juice, and cognac until well blended. Add cold chicken cubes. Fold in remaining ingredients. Serve on lettuce leaves or water cress. Makes 4 servings.

Chicken Pickle Aspic Dryone

Here's a clever and tasty way to use leftover chicken stock.

2 tablespoons unflavored gelatin	6 strips pimiento
1 cup cold chicken stock	6 strips sweet pickle
5 cups hot chicken stock	6 black olives
2 cups chopped sweet pickle	

Soften gelatin in cold chicken stock; dissolve in boiling stock, stirring well. Chill gelatin until slightly thickened and syrupy. Fold in chopped pickles; turn into a 1-quart mold. Chill overnight. Unmold on a platter and garnish with remaining ingredients. Makes 4 servings.

Chicken Turnovers Alex

An adaptation of the Russian turnovers with saffron as a new ingredient.

1 cup ground cooked chicken	¼ teaspoon rosemary
6 slices white bread, crusts removed	⅛ teaspoon ginger
1 egg yolk, slightly beaten	dash powdered saffron
1 small clove garlic, minced	1 tablespoon lemon juice
2 tablespoons chopped onion	dash Tabasco
1 tablespoon chopped parsley	1 teaspoon salt
1 tablespoon chopped celery	⅛ teaspoon pepper
¼ cup chopped stuffed green olives	1 package instant pie crust mix

Heat oven to 400°F. Chill chicken 10 minutes. Cover bread with water; let stand 1 minute. Squeeze out water. Mash bread and mix with chicken, egg yolk, garlic, onion, parsley, celery, olives, spices, and combined lemon juice and seasonings. Prepare pie crust mix according to directions on package. Roll pastry to ⅛ inch thick. Cut in 2-inch squares for canapés, or 6-inch squares for luncheon turnovers. Divide filling among squares, placing it in center of each. Fold squares into triangles. Brush edges with water, press together, and crimp edges with fork. Brush tops with milk or unbeaten egg white. Bake 8 to 10 minutes for small turnovers, 12 to 15 minutes for larger ones. Makes 18 small or 8 large turnovers.

TURKEY

ROAST TURKEY—ONE

Turkey is no longer reserved for Christmas or Thanksgiving. Plan to serve it often and prove to your family that some of the best meals are inspired by planning leftovers. Plan three gala meals for eight servings each with one turkey.

MEAL NO. 1

Roast Turkey with Sage Stuffing

Sweet Potato Casserole
Creamed Onions   Buttered Carrots
Green Goddess Salad
Pumpkin Pie
Mince Pie

MEAL NO. 2

Turkey à la King Beaujolais

Whipped Potatoes   Peas and Onions
Cranberry and Pineapple Relish
Tomato and Cucumber Salad
Apple Pie à la Mode

MEAL NO. 3

Aztec Turkey Molé

Saffron Rice   Buttered Broccoli
Sliced Tomatoes
Relishes
Fruit Cocktail

Roast Turkey with Sage Stuffing

turkey neck, wing tips, and giblets	10- to 12-pound turkey
1 onion	2 tablespoons butter, melted
1 stalk celery	3 tablespoons lemon juice
1 quart water	Sage Stuffing (*see below*)
2 teaspoons salt	1 cup dry white wine
½ teaspoon pepper	1 tablespoon flour

To make stock, wash neck, wing tips, and giblets and place in a large, heavy kettle with onion, celery, water, 1 teaspoon of the salt, and ¼ teaspoon of the pepper. Cover and cook until meat falls from neck bones, about 1½ hours. Strain and reserve stock. Reserve giblets to add to gravy, if desired.

While stock is cooking, wash turkey inside and out and dry well. Rub it with melted butter. Sprinkle with the remaining salt and pepper and the lemon juice. Prepare stuffing. Stuff and truss turkey and tie the legs together. Heat oven to 325°F. Place turkey on a rack in a roasting pan, cover with aluminum foil, and bake 1½ hours. Remove turkey from rack and return to pan. Pour wine over it, cover again, and continue roasting 2 hours. Pour 2 cups of the reserved stock into a saucepan. Combine flour and another ¼ cup stock and add flour mixture to stock in saucepan. Bring to a boil and simmer 5 minutes, stirring constantly.

Skim fat from roasting pan. Pour thickened stock over turkey. Increase oven temperature to 375°F. and continue baking, uncovered, another 30 minutes or until nicely browned. Baste frequently. Remove turkey to a serving platter. Serve the pan gravy in a gravy boat. Makes 8 servings with leftovers.

Sage Stuffing

1 cup butter	1 teaspoon salt
½ cup chopped onion	½ teaspoon pepper
1 cup chopped celery	2 teaspoons ground sage
8 cups small bread cubes, toasted	½ cup turkey stock
¼ cup chopped parsley	

Melt butter in a heavy skillet. Add onion and celery and sauté until onion is golden. Combine bread cubes, parsley, salt, pepper, and sage in a large mixing bowl. Add sautéed mixture and toss stuffing lightly with two forks to mix well. Add turkey stock and toss again.

Turkey à la King Beaujolais

1 can (6 ounces) sliced mushrooms, drained
½ cup diced green pepper
½ cup margarine
7 tablespoons flour
¾ teaspoon salt
¼ teaspoon celery salt
⅛ teaspoon pepper
⅛ teaspoon paprika
2 cups canned chicken broth
1½ cups light cream
½ cup heavy cream
2 cups cooked, cubed turkey
¼ cup chopped pimiento
2 tablespoons Beaujolais wine
8 baked patty shells

Sauté mushrooms and green pepper in margarine for 5 minutes. Remove from heat. Blend in flour, salts, pepper, and paprika. Cook over low heat, stirring constantly, until mixture is bubbly. Remove from heat. Slowly stir in broth and creams. Heat mixture to boiling, stirring constantly; boil 1 minute. Add turkey, pimiento, and wine; heat 4 minutes. Serve hot in patty shells. Makes 8 servings.

Aztec Turkey Molé

2 green peppers, cut and seeded
2 small onions, peeled
2 cans (1 pound each) tomatoes
1 can (4 ounces) pimiento, drained
¼ cup blanched almonds
¼ cup pecans
¼ cup vegetable oil
1 tablespoon chili powder
1¼ teaspoons salt
¼ teaspoon Tabasco
¼ teaspoon Worcestershire sauce
⅛ teaspoon ground cinnamon
⅛ teaspoon ground cloves
2 chicken bouillon cubes
¼ cup fine dry bread crumbs
1 square (1 ounce) unsweetened chocolate
8 large slices cooked turkey

Heat oven to 350°F. Put peppers, onions, tomatoes, pimiento, almonds, and pecans in electric blender; blend until smooth. Heat oil in a large, heavy skillet. Add blended mixture, seasonings, and bouillon cubes. Bring to a boil. Reduce heat, cover, and simmer 30 minutes. Stir in bread crumbs and chocolate. Heat, stirring occasionally, until chocolate is melted. Make alternate layers of turkey slices and mixture in a 2½-quart casserole. Bake 20 minutes. Makes 8 servings.

ROAST TURKEY—TWO

In the Near East, turkey is stuffed with ground meat to make an unusually flavored stuffing. A 10-pound turkey or even a slightly smaller one will yield three delicious meals.

MEAL NO. 1

Oriental Stuffed Turkey

Pan-browned Potatoes   Stewed Celery
Glazed Carrots
Cranberry Sauce   Romaine Salad
Cherry Cobbler with Hard Sauce

MEAL NO. 2

Turkey Roll-Ups

Buttered Peas   Lima Beans and Bacon
Pineapple Salad
Stewed Pears with Marmalade

MEAL NO. 3

Turkey Bisque Madeleine

French-toasted Ham and Cheese Sandwiches
Raw Spinach Salad
Orange Relish
Applesauce Cake

Oriental Stuffed Turkey

The dining room of the Imperial Hotel in Yokohama served this superb meat-stuffed turkey when I was there recently.

turkey neck, wing tips, and giblets
1 onion
1 stalk celery
1 quart water
1¾ teaspoons salt
⅜ teaspoon pepper
9- to 10-pound turkey

2 tablespoons butter, melted
2 tablespoons lemon juice
Oriental Ground Meat Stuffing
   (*see below*)
1 cup dry white wine
1 tablespoon flour

Follow method of preparation of Roast Turkey with Sage Stuffing (page89).

Oriental Ground Meat Stuffing

2 tablespoons butter	¾ pound chestnuts, roasted and
1 small onion, grated	chopped
1 pound lean ground beef	1 cup dry toasted crumbs
½ cup dry white wine	3 tablespoons currants
1 tablespoon tomato sauce	2 tablespoons chopped parsley
1 teaspoon salt	½ teaspoon sage
¼ teaspoon pepper	¼ teaspoon basil
¼ cup pignolia nuts	¼ teaspoon oregano

Melt butter in a heavy skillet; add onion and meat and sauté until lightly browned. Add wine, tomato sauce, salt, and pepper. Cover and simmer 15 minutes. Skim off any fat. Add remaining ingredients and mix well. Cool thoroughly before stuffing turkey.

Turkey Roll-Ups

A casserole with contrasting flavors, easily put together.

2 tablespoons chopped onion	12 large thin slices cooked turkey
½ cup butter or margarine	½ cup slivered toasted almonds
2½ cups cooked potatoes, diced	2 teaspoons steak sauce
1½ cups cooked, drained spinach	1 teaspoon Worcestershire sauce
dash of white pepper	

Heat oven to 350°F. Sauté onion in 2 tablespoons of the butter until transparent. Remove from heat and add potatoes, spinach, and pepper. Toss together lightly. Spoon some of the mixture in the center of each turkey slice; fold ends over and secure with wooden pick. Place roll-ups in a 1½-quart casserole. Melt the remaining butter, stir in the almonds, steak sauce, and Worcestershire sauce. Pour over the roll-ups. Bake 25 minutes or until lightly browned. Makes 6 servings.

Turkey Bisque Madeleine

3 tablespoons butter or margarine	dash of nutmeg
3 tablespoons flour	dash of mace
2½ cups turkey broth or canned	½ teaspoon salt
chicken broth	⅛ teaspoon pepper
½ cup sauterne	⅛ teaspoon paprika
1 cup cooked ground turkey	1 tablespoon chopped parsley
1 cup light cream	1 teaspoon chopped chives
1 tablespoon sherry	

Melt butter in a skillet; stir in flour. Add broth, sauterne, and turkey; cook, stirring constantly, until mixture boils and thickens. Simmer 5 minutes. Add cream, sherry, nutmeg, mace, salt, pepper, and paprika. Heat until piping hot. Pour into heated soup bowls or cups; garnish each serving with a sprinkling of parsley and chives. Makes 4½ cups or 6 to 8 servings.

ROAST TURKEY—THREE

A 9- to 10-pound turkey can yield many interesting meals which need not just be heated up or eaten cold as leftovers. Use the cooked meat as an ingredient in a delicious main dish and it will take on new importance.

MEAL NO. 1

Pilgrim's Roast Turkey with Chestnut Stuffing

Whipped Parslied Potatoes
Green Peas and White Onions
Cranberry Sauce
Celery, Walnut, and Pimiento Salad
Orange Sherbet

MEAL NO. 2

Steamboat Turkey Balls

Fluffy Saffron Rice
Glazed Carrots   Waldorf Salad
Chocolate Eclairs

MEAL NO. 3

The Captain's Turkey Chowder

Cheese Soufflé
Tossed Green Salad
Buttered French Bread Chunks
Coconut Cream Pie

MEAL NO. 4

Turkey Tetrazzini

Buttered Broccoli Spears
Spiced Apple Wedges
Chocolate Brownie à la Mode

Pilgrim's Roast Turkey with Chestnut Stuffing

9½ -pound turkey
½ cup chopped onions
¼ cup chopped green onions
2 tablespoons butter
½ pound sausage meat
turkey liver, coarsely chopped
2¼ cups dry bread crumbs
¼ teaspoon thyme
¼ teaspoon marjoram

3 tablespoons finely chopped parsley
1 teaspoon finely chopped celery
2 teaspoons salt
¼ teaspoon pepper
¼ teaspoon paprika
1 teaspoon lemon juice
20 cooked chestnuts, peeled
¼ cup heavy cream
3 tablespoons margarine, softened

Wash turkey thoroughly and dry well inside and out. To make the stuffing, sauté onions in butter until lightly browned. Stir in sausage meat and turkey liver; cook 5 minutes. Stir in bread crumbs, thyme, marjoram, parsley, celery, seasonings, and lemon juice; mix lightly. Purée chestnuts in a sieve; add to mixture. Moisten with heavy cream. Heat oven to 350°F. Stuff turkey. Rub turkey with softened margarine; set on rack in roasting pan. Roast 4 to 4½ hours, basting frequently with pan drippings. When turkey is done, let stand 15 minutes before carving. Make gravy with drippings. Makes 6 servings with turkey left over.

Steamboat Turkey Balls

The old riverboat menus featured this dish quite often.

½ cup white wine
½ cup water
¼ teaspoon salt
12 oysters
1 cup finely chopped cooked turkey
1 tablespoon finely chopped green
     onions
2 tablespoons butter
4 egg yolks

1 teaspoon lemon juice
¼ cup heavy cream
¼ teaspoon salt
¼ teaspoon onion salt
½ teaspoon Tabasco
1 tablespoon finely chopped celery
½ cup dry bread crumbs
½ cup ground pecans
shortening for frying

Combine wine, water, and salt in a medium saucepan. Bring to a boil, then reduce heat to simmering. Add oysters and simmer for 2 minutes. Remove oysters; chop finely. Combine with turkey. Sauté green onions in butter until transparent; add to turkey mixture. Add 2 of the egg yolks, lemon juice, 2 tablespoons of the heavy cream, salts, Tabasco, and celery; mix well. Shape into ¾-inch balls; chill 1 hour. Combine remaining egg yolks with remaining cream. Combine bread crumbs with pecans. Dip balls in egg-yolk mixture; roll in crumbs and pecan mixture; chill 1 hour. Fry a few balls at a time in deep fat, at 375°F. Cook until delicately browned on all sides; drain on absorbent paper. Makes 6 servings.

The Captain's Turkey Chowder

A flavorful soup ideally suited for a midnight snack, served with chunks of French bread.

1 medium onion, chopped	½ teaspoon pepper
¼ cup finely chopped celery	turkey carcass, cut in pieces
6 mushrooms, chopped	2 cups milk
2 tablespoons butter	1 cup light cream
4 cups boiling water	2 tablespoons finely chopped
¼ cup rice	parsley
1½ teaspoons salt	

Sauté onion, celery, and mushrooms in butter 5 minutes or until onion is golden, in a large, heavy saucepan. Add boiling water, rice, seasonings, and turkey carcass. Cover saucepan. Heat to boiling; simmer 30 minutes or until rice is tender. Remove bones. Scrape off meat and return to soup. Add milk and cream; heat thoroughly but do not boil. Serve with a sprinkling of parsley. Makes 6 servings.

Turkey Tetrazzini

Another version of the ever-popular Italian dish.

½ cup turkey or chicken broth	¾ package (8 ounces) spaghetti, cooked according to package directions
1 can (10½ ounces) condensed cream of mushroom soup	
1 tablespoon steak sauce	2 cups diced cooked turkey
½ teaspoon Worcestershire sauce	2 tablespoons slivered almonds
1 cup shredded Cheddar cheese	2 tablespoons chopped pecans
1 can (2 counces) mushroom stems and pieces, drained	¼ cup grated Romano cheese

Heat oven to 350°F. Blend broth, mushroom soup, steak sauce and Worcestershire sauce; stir in remaining ingredients except Romano cheese. Pour into a 1½-quart baking dish; sprinkle with cheese. Bake 30 minutes. Makes 4 servings.

DUCK

ROAST DUCK

If your hunter comes home with ducks, try these different menus which will add a piquancy to each dish and make your husband happy that he brought his prizes home.

MEAL NO. 1

Duck Casserole Chasseur

Green Goddess Salad
French Bread with Garlic Butter
Lemon Chiffon Pie

MEAL NO. 2

Germain's Duck Soup

Grilled Ham and Swiss Cheese Sandwiches
Marinated Vegetable Salad
Fresh Fruit Wedges

MEAL NO. 3

Duck Del Sol

Creamed Spinach
Saffron Rice   Jellied Salad
Mint Parfait

Duck Casserole Chasseur

2 medium ducks, skinned and
cut up
1 teaspoon salt
½ teaspoon pepper
⅛ teaspoon thyme
⅛ teaspoon sage
4 teaspoons ground ginger
4 tablespoons butter
2 green onions, chopped
1 pound fresh mushrooms

1½ cups rice
1 package (10 ounces) frozen peas
1½ cups claret wine
1½ cups chicken broth
1 teaspoon chervil
½ teaspoon marjoram
½ teaspoon rosemary
2 medium tomatoes, chopped
1 teaspoon onion salt

Heat oven to 325°F. Rub duck pieces with mixture of salt, pepper, thyme, sage, and ginger; brown in the butter in a heavy skillet over high heat. Remove duck to a heavy 5-quart casserole. Pour off excess fat and in the same skillet sauté onions and mushrooms 5 minutes. Add to duck pieces. Bake 1 hour. Remove duck to a heated platter. Pour off all accumulated fat from casserole. Place rice in bottom of casserole. Add duck, peas, wine, broth, seasonings, tomatoes, and onion salt. Cover. Increase heat oven to 350°F. and bake 45 minutes. Makes 6 servings.

Germain's Duck Soup

carcasses of ducks, cut in pieces
7 cups water
3 stalks celery, cut up
1 carrot, sliced
1 small turnip, sliced

1 teaspoon minced parsley
¾ teaspoon salt
¼ teaspoon pepper
2 cups cooked rice

Put duck carcasses in a large kettle with water, celery, carrot, turnip, and parsley. Heat to boiling; reduce heat and skim top. Cover and simmer 2 hours. Strain. Skim off excess fat. Add any bits of duck meat from bones. Season with salt and pepper, stir in rice, and reheat. Makes 8 servings.

Duck Del Sol

2 tablespoons sherry
1 cup ground cooked duck meat
¾ cup milk
1 cup soft bread crumbs
1 teaspoon minced shallot
1 teaspoon minced parsley

1 teaspoon minced celery
½ teaspoon salt
⅛ teaspoon pepper
½ teaspoon nutmeg
3 egg whites, stiffly beaten

Pour wine over meat and let stand. Heat oven to 375°F. Pour milk over bread crumbs in a medium saucepan; cook over low heat 5 minutes. Combine crumb mixture with duck meat, shallot, parsley, celery, and seasonings. Gently fold in egg whites. Turn into a well-buttered, 4-cup ring mold. Set in a pan of hot water. Bake 30 minutes or until top is firm to the touch. Let stand 1 minute. Unmold on a heated platter. Makes 6 servings.

GOOSE

ROAST GOOSE

Buy a 10- to 12-pound goose and plan to have two meals. Plan on ¾ pound per person to be served for the main meal.

MEAL NO. 1

Roast Goose Provençale

*Wild Rice Limores
Orange-Cranberry Relish
Gingered Carrots
Avocado and Pecan Salad
Top Plum Pudding

MEAL NO. 2

Taj Mahal Salad

French Fried Potatoes   Hot Garlic Rolls
Baba au Rhum

Roast Goose Provençale

The traditional paysanne goose served during the holidays.

10- to 12-pound goose
6 tablespoons butter
3 medium onions, chopped
3 celery stalks, chopped
½ teaspoon thyme
½ teaspoon sage
¼ teaspoon basil

¼ teaspoon oregano
2 teaspoons salt
7 cups soft white bread crumbs
1½ tablespoons minced parsley
2 medium apples, pared, cored, finely chopped

Wipe goose with a damp cloth; remove large layers of fat from inside goose. Heat oven to 300°F. To make the stuffing, melt butter in a large, heavy skillet. Add onions and celery; sauté 5 minutes or until tender but not browned. Stir in seasonings. Combine bread crumbs, parsley, and apples. Pour seasoned mixture over crumb mixture and blend well. Stuff goose and truss it. Place on rack, breast down, in a roasting pan and bake 30 minutes to the pound. Add 1 cup water while it roasts. Remove fat from roasting pan and make gravy from pan drippings. Add chopped cooked giblets to gravy, if desired. Makes 6 servings.

Wild Rice Limores

heart, neck, gizzard, and liver of goose	1 bay leaf
1 onion, chopped	1 quart water
2 stalks celery, sliced	2 cups wild rice
1 teaspoon salt	1 teaspoon onion salt

Simmer together heart, neck, gizzard (add liver last 15 minutes of cooking), onion, celery, salt, and bay leaf in water for 2½ hours. Strain broth; discard bones and vegetables. Chop giblets and set aside for gravy. Wash rice until water is almost clear. Soak in cold water 1 hour. Drain. Measure 4 cups giblet broth in a medium saucepan; add wild rice and onion salt. Bring to boil. Cover; reduce heat and cook 30 minutes or until tender. Makes 6 servings.

Taj Mahal Salad

2 cups diced cooked goose	⅛ teaspoon pepper
1 tablespoon tarragon vinegar	dash paprika
½ teaspoon minced onion	dash nutmeg
½ teaspoon dry mustard	1 medium avocado, pared, diced
¼ cup mayonnaise	1 large orange, peeled, sliced, cut into bite-sized pieces
¾ cup commercial sour cream	
¼ cup chutney, coarsely chopped	crisp lettuce leaves
½ teaspoon salt	6 lime slices

Remove all fat from goose meat. Blend vinegar, onion, and mustard into a smooth paste. Blend with mayonnaise, sour cream, and chutney. Add seasonings; let stand 1 hour. Add dressing to mixture of goose meat, avocado, and orange, tossing lightly. Chill 1 hour. Serve on crisp lettuce leaves. Garnish with lime slices. Makes 6 servings.

FISH

RED SNAPPER

A whole red snapper may tempt you to plan some fish meals as a change of pace. The unusual Delphi Mold may be served as a first course at a formal dinner.

MEAL NO.1

Baked Fish au Vin

Twice-baked Potatoes
Silced Eggs on Romaine
Nesselrode Pie

MEAL NO. 2

Delphi Mold

Beef Fillett Niçoise
Buttered Zucchini Circles
Grapefruit and Avocado Salad
Boston Cream Pie

MEAL NO. 3

Eastern Fish Chowder

Egg and Minced Ham Sandwiches
Salad with Creamy Italian Dressing
Apple Cupcakes

Baked Fish au Vin

6 tablespoons olive oil
6- to 7-pound red snapper
½ cup dry white wine
juice of 1 lemon
1½ teaspoons salt
¼ teaspoon pepper

½ pound fresh spinach
12 to 14 green onions, chopped
1 large onion, chopped
2 cups canned tomatoes
¼ cup dark currants

Heat oven to 350°F. Pour 1 tablespoon of the olive oil in bottom of a shallow baking dish large enough to accommodate fish. Arrange fish in pan. Pour wine over it. Sprinkle with lemon juice and season with salt and pepper. Bake 15 minutes. Wilt spinach in boiling water; drain. In a heavy skillet heat remaining olive oil; add green onions and onion; sauté until lightly browned. Add spinach; cook 3 minutes. Add tomatoes and currants; cook 12 minutes. Remove fish from oven; spread vegetables over it. Return to oven; bake 45 minutes longer. If sauce becomes watery, thicken with flour paste, cook 10 minutes more. Remove fish carefully onto a heated platter. Makes 6 servings.

Delphi Mold

An elegant cold party dish, ideal for buffet serving.

⅔ cup cream cheese, mashed
½ cup grated American Cheddar cheese, mashed
1 cup crumbled Roquefort cheese, mashed
2 tablespoons unflavored gelatin
juice of 1 lemon, strained
½ cup boiling water
½ teaspoon salt

2 cups heavy cream, whipped
½ cup minced chives
2 cups leftover cooked fish
1 cup celery, cut into 1-inch pieces
½ cup mayonnaise
¼ cup heavy cream
2 tablespoons chopped parsley
lettuce or water cress

Combine cheeses; set aside. Soak gelatin in lemon juice; dissolve in boiling water. Stir cheeses into gelatin. Add salt. Fold in whipped cream and chives. Turn into a 2-quart ring mold; chill overnight. Combine remaining ingredients. Unmold cheese ring on a platter garnished with crisp lettuce leaves or water cress; fill center with fish mixture. Makes 6 servings.

Eastern Fish Chowder

2 cups cooked fish, coarsely flaked
5 strips crisp bacon, chopped
1 onion, chopped
2 cups potatoes, pared, diced
1 cup water
1 can (10½ ounces) condensed cream of celery soup

1 can (10½ ounces) condensed New England-style clam chowder
2 cups milk
1 cup light cream
1 teaspoon salt
¼ teaspoon pepper
3 tablespoons minced parsley

Keep fish refrigerated until needed. In bacon fat, cook the onion until tender but not browned. Add potatoes; fry 4 minutes. Add water, soups, milk, and cream; stir until well blended. Season with salt and pepper. Gently stir in fish and bacon bits. Stir in ½ the parsley. Heat until piping hot. Pour into a large soup tureen; sprinkle with remaining parsley and serve hot. Makes 6 servings.

FILLET OF SOLE

Frozen or fresh fish can be served in many tempting ways. Try these fillet of sole specialties next time you want something different.

MEAL NO. 1

Fillet of Sole à la Française

Fluffy Rice
Creamed Spinach
Cucumber and Chicory Salad
Strawberry Pie

MEAL NO. 2

Broiled Fish à la Grecque

*Lemon Sauce
Artichokes   Baby Carrots
Endive and Water Cress Salad
Cream Puffs

MEAL NO. 3

Fish Pie Devonshire

Buttered Lima Beans
Green Beans with Mushrooms
Orange Gelatin Salad
Cupcakes

Fillet of Sole à la Française

2 teaspoons butter
2 pounds fillet of sole
½ cup bottled clam juice
1 cup dry white wine
1 cup canned tomatoes, drained, mashed
4 tablespoons minced parsley
1 tablespoon minced celery

4 tablespoons minced shallots
2 tablespoons minced green onion tops
½ teaspoon thyme
¼ teaspoon rosemary
¼ teaspoon basil
6 tablespoons butter

Melt the 2 teaspoons butter in a large, heavy skillet. Roll each fillet into a ball and secure with wooden picks. Place fillets in skillet; pour in clam juice and wine. Simmer 2 minutes. Add tomatoes, parsley, celery, shallots, green onion tops, thyme, rosemary, and basil. Simmer 10 minutes longer. Remove fish to a heated serving platter. Remove wooden picks. Boil sauce in skillet 3 or 4 minutes. Stir in the 6 tablespoons butter and blend well. Pour over fish and serve. Makes 4 servings.

Broiled Fish à la Grecque

The Grecian way of serving fish with a Lemon Sauce.

4 pounds fillet of sole
1½ teaspoons salt
¼ teaspoon pepper

1 cup Lemon Sauce (*see below*), heated

Sprinkle fish with salt and pepper. Place on aluminum foil on broiler rack. Brush with hot Lemon Sauce. Broil 5 minutes on each side or until thoroughly cooked, basting fish frequently with Lemon Sauce. Place on a heated platter; pour balance of sauce over fish. Makes 8 servings.

Lemon Sauce

½ cup olive oil
½ cup lemon juice
1 teaspoon oregano

pinch of sage
½ teaspoon salt

Combine all ingredients in a covered jar; shake well. Makes 1 cup.

Fish Pie Devonshire

The English are famous for their pastries and pies; this fish pie is a sophisticated favorite of the Soho.

2½ tablespoons butter	¼ teaspoon pepper
2 medium onions, sliced	1 egg, well beaten
2 cups cooked fish	2 cups mashed potatoes
2 hard-cooked eggs, sliced	1 tablespoon chopped parsley
2 small tomatoes, peeled, sliced	2 tablespoons chopped almonds
1 teaspoon salt	

Heat oven to 400°F. Heat 1 tablespoon of the butter in a skillet; add onions and sauté until lightly browned. Stir in fish; mix gently. Melt another ½ tablespoon butter in a 1-quart baking dish. Lay in slices of egg and tomato and top with fish mixture, repeating until all these ingredients are used. Season to taste. Mix ¾ the beaten egg with the mashed potatoes, parsley, and almonds. Spread over top of baking dish. Dot with remaining butter and brush with remaining egg. Bake 25 minutes or until top is well browned. Makes 4 servings.

HADDOCK

Sometimes fresh fish looks so tempting that you cannot resist buying more than you need for one meal. Here we show you how to use haddock in three deliciously different meals.

MEAL NO. 1

Fish of the Islands

Spinach Soufflé   Baked Potatoes
Caesar Salad
Banana Cream Pie

MEAL NO. 2

Harry's Haddock Hash

Broiled Tomatoes   Buttered Chick Peas
Romaine Salad
Marble Cake

MEAL NO. 3

New Way Fish Roll

Succotash   Creamed Peas
Cucumber Salad
Ice Cream Pie

Fish of the Islands

2 pounds boned, skinned haddock
1 teaspoon salt
1 cup lime juice
2 tablespoons grated fresh coconut
1 cup prepared French dressing
2 hard-cooked eggs, sliced
1 tablespoon chopped parsley

Cut fish into 1-inch squares. Place fish squares in a shallow heatproof dish and sprinkle with salt and lime juice. Let stand 4 hours. Add coconut to French dressing. Drain fish and discard lime juice. Pour French dressing over fish. Simmer 10 minutes. Serve with garnish of egg slices and parsley. Makes 4 servings.

Harry's Haddock Hash

Harry was a San Francisco character who enjoyed cooking. The story goes that he improvised this fish hash because he never ate meat.

1 cup coarsely flaked cooked
    haddock
1 cup chopped boiled potatoes
1 teaspoon chopped parsley
1 teaspoon chopped green pepper
½ teaspoon salt
⅛ teaspoon pepper
dash cayenne
dash Tabasco
pinch nutmeg
1 tablespoon butter

Mix fish and potatoes lightly; add parsley, green pepper, and seasonings. Heat butter in a medium skillet. Add fish mixture; brown lightly over medium heat, stirring with a fork. Pat mixture lightly and continue cooking until well browned on bottom. Fold over and slide onto a heated platter. Makes 4 servings.

New Way Fish Roll

2 tablespoons butter	¼ cup diced celery
2 tablespoons chopped onion	1 cup cooked haddock
2 tablespoons flour	¾ teaspoon salt
¾ cup light cream	⅛ teaspoon pepper
1 tablespoon minced parsley	⅛ teaspoon paprika
1 tablespoon minced celery	1 recipe Herb Biscuits, page 117

Heat oven to 425°F. Melt butter in a skillet; add onion and sauté until slightly browned. Stir in flour and cook 1 minute. Gradually add cream, stirring constantly until thickened and smooth. Remove from heat. Add parsley, celery, haddock, and seasonings. Roll out biscuit dough on a floured surface into a rectangle ½ inch thick. Spread fish mixture over dough. Roll up like a jelly roll. With greased, sharp knife cut roll into 1-inch slices. Place on a greased cookie sheet. Bake 12 to 15 minutes or until well browned. Makes 4 servings.

FISH FILLETS

If you bought more fish than you planned to use, don't despair. Cook it all in a rich curry, serve as much as needed and plan to use the balance in other meals.

MEAL NO. 1

Fish Curry Hawaiian

Fluffy Rice   Creamed Spinach
Cabbage-Carrot Slaw
Spiced Bananas and Grapes
Cookies

MEAL NO. 2

Kedgeree

Brussels Sprouts
Apple, Banana, and Date Salad
Plantation Cake

MEAL NO. 3

Fish Coladone

French Fried Potatoes
Buttered Broccoli
Wilted Greens Salad
Chocolate Cake

Fish Curry Hawaiian

½ cup vegetable oil
4 medium onions, chopped
2 tablespoons curry powder
1 teaspoon paprika
1 teaspoon pepper

1½ teaspoons salt
1 cup tomato sauce
4 cups hot water
3 pounds fish fillets

Heat oil in a large, heavy saucepan; add onions, curry powder, paprika, pepper, and salt and brown lightly. Add tomato sauce. Cook over moderate heat, stirring constantly, 15 minutes or until almost dry. Stir in hot water. Simmer 20 minutes. Add fish and simmer 15 minutes or until tender. Serve at once. Makes 6 servings.

Kedgeree

The English colonials in nineteenth-century India had about a dozen ways of serving this delicious dish. Here is one of my favorites.

1 tablespoon butter
2 tablespoons minced onion
1 cup cooked rice
1 tablespoon minced parsley
1 teaspoon minced green pepper

1 teaspoon curry powder
½ teaspoon Worcestershire sauce
1 cup cooked fish curry fillet, flaked
2 tablespoons sherry

Melt butter in a medium skillet; add onion and sauté until tender. Stir in rice, parsley, green pepper, curry powder, and Worcestershire sauce. Blend well and cook 2 minutes. Remove from heat. Let stand 15 minutes. Heat oven to 400°F. Turn fish into a greased 1-quart baking dish. Pour sherry over it. Top with rice mixture. Bake 20 minutes or until bubbly hot. Makes 4 servings.

Fish Coladone

6 hard-cooked eggs
¼ cup leftover fish curry fillets
1 teaspoon prepared mustard
dash cayenne
¼ teaspoon curry powder
mayonnaise
2 tablespoons butter

2 tablespoons flour
½ cup light cream
½ cup milk
½ teaspoon salt
⅛ teaspoon pepper
¼ cup grated sharp Cheddar cheese
1 egg yolk, lightly beaten

Heat oven to 375°F. Slit eggs lengthwise; remove yolks to a mixing bowl and mash thoroughly. Add fish, prepared mustard, cayenne, and curry powder and mix well. Add enough mayonnaise to hold mixture together. Stuff egg whites with mixture. Place in a greased, shallow baking dish. Melt butter in a saucepan; stir in flour until smooth. Stir in cream and milk. Season with salt and pepper. Cook, stirring constantly, until thickened. Stir in cheese and egg yolk. Pour over stuffed eggs. Bake 15 minutes or until lightly browned. Makes 4 servings.

THE
LEFTOVERS

VEGETABLES

Winter Garden Loaf

A dramatic salad mold, refreshing and delicious.

2 packages lemon-flavored gelatin
3½ cups hot water
3 tablespoons vinegar
¼ teaspoon salt
¼ teaspoon seasoned salt
16 canned whole green beans
4 long strips pimiento

1 cup cooked cauliflowerets
¼ cup cooked sliced carrots
¼ cup cooked, diced green pepper
¼ cup diced celery
¼ cup sliced radishes
¼ cup sliced green onions
lettuce leaves

Dissolve gelatin in hot water; add vinegar and salts. Pour about ½ inch gelatin mixture in an 8½ x 4½ x 2½-inch loaf pan. Chill until set. Divide beans in bundles of 4. Circle each bundle with a pimiento strip. Arrange on gelatin in pan. Chill remaining gelatin until partially set; pour enough over beans to cover. Chill until firm. Combine remaining gelatin with remaining vegetables. Pour over firm gelatin in pan; chill until set. Unmold on bed of lettuce. Makes 8 servings.

Fried Rollies

2 eggs, separated
2 cups leftover mashed potatoes
¼ pound processed American cheese, cubed
1 teaspoon baking powder
½ teaspoon curry powder

⅛ teaspoon garlic salt
¼ teaspoon paprika
2 tablespoons water
1 cup fine bread crumbs
shortening for frying

Add egg yolks to mashed potatoes; mix well. Add cheese, baking powder, and seasonings. Form into 12 1-inch balls. Combine egg whites with water. Dip balls into egg white mixture. Roll in bread crumbs. Fry in hot shortening , 375°F., 4 minutes or until golden brown. Serve hot. Makes 4 servings.

Potato Cups Madeleine

3 cups leftover mashed potatoes
melted butter
1 can (8 ounces) cheese sauce

2 strips bacon, crisp-fried, crumbled
6 strips pimiento

Heat oven to 400°F. Shape mashed potatoes into 6 mounds on a greased baking sheet. Make a hollow in the center of each mound with a tablespoon; brush with melted butter. Bake 10 minutes. Fill mounds with cheese sauce; place under broiler for a few minutes to brown. Sprinkle with bacon; decorate with pimiento. Serve hot. Makes 6 servings.

Chantilly Potato Cups

2 cups leftover mashed potatoes
1 egg yolk
2 tablespoons butter
¼ cup finely chopped green pepper
2 tablespoons finely chopped onion
½ teaspoon salt

⅛ teaspoon pepper
⅛ teaspoon paprika
½ cup heavy cream
¼ cup grated cheese
1 egg white, stiffly beaten

Heat oven to 350°F. Combine potatoes and egg yolk and blend well. Melt butter in a skillet. Add green pepper and onion and cook over low heat until tender. Add to mashed potatoes and mix well. Season mixture with salt, pepper, and paprika. Spoon mixture into 6 greased custard cups. Whip cream until stiff. Fold in cheese and egg white. Spoon over potato mixture. Bake 30 minutes or until a knife inserted in the center comes out clean. Serve immediately. Makes 6 servings.

Cordon Bleu Pancakes

1½ cups cold mashed potatoes
3 tablespoons flour
¾ teaspoon salt
⅛ teaspoon pepper

⅛ teaspoon paprika
½ cup chopped Bleu cheese
butter

Mix potatoes, flour, and seasonings. Shape into 8 thin patties about 2 inches wide. Sprinkle 4 patties with cheese; cover with remaining patties. Press together to thoroughly enclose cheese. Sauté over low heat in a small amount of butter until browned on both sides. Makes 4 servings.

Pink Luncheon Salad

1 cup slivered cooked beets
2 cups coarsely chopped celery
1 teaspoon instant minced onion

¼ cup French dressing
1 teaspoon sesame seed
salad greens

Combine beets and celery in a bowl. Mix onion, dressing, and sesame seed; add to beet mixture and toss lightly. Chill and serve on salad greens. Makes 4 servings.

Carrots Louisa

1½ cups diced cooked carrots
3 soda crackers, crushed
½ teaspoon onion salt
2 tablespoons chopped green pepper

⅛ teaspoon pepper
1 tablespoon butter, melted
¼ cup grated sharp cheese

Heat oven to 425°F. Grease a 1-quart baking dish. Place a layer of carrots in the bottom. Combine crackers, onion salt, green pepper, and pepper. Spread mixture over carrots and alternate layers until all ingredients are used. Pour butter over mixture and sprinkle with cheese. Bake 15 to 20 minutes or until cheese melts. Makes 4 servings.

Peas and Celery au Coq

2 cups sliced celery
1 teaspoon instant minced onion
½ cup chicken broth
2 teaspoons flour
¼ cup light cream

1 to 1½ cups leftover cooked peas
1 tablespoon butter
½ teaspoon salt
⅛ teaspoon pepper

Combine celery, onion, and chicken broth in a medium saucepan; cover and simmer 15 minutes. Blend flour and cream; stir into mixture. Cook, stirring constantly, until slightly thickened. Add peas and butter. Heat 2 minutes. Season with salt and pepper. Makes 4 servings.

Frankfurters à la Patoush

6 strips bacon
6 frankfurters
1½ cups leftover mashed potatoes
1 egg
1½ tablespoons chopped onion

½ teaspoon celery salt
⅛ teaspoon paprika
1 teaspoon prepared mustard
2 teaspoons horseradish

Heat oven to 425°F. Fry bacon until limp. Cut frankfurters almost through lengthwise; lay open. Mix together remaining ingredients. Spoon potato mixture into frankfurters; close halves. Wrap each frankfurter with bacon and fasten with wooden pick. Place in shallow baking pan. Bake 10 to 15 minutes or until bacon is crisp. Makes 6 servings.

Puff and Bacon

4 strips bacon
¾ cup milk
¾ cup grated American cheese
½ teaspoon Worcestershire sauce
dash Tabasco

¼ teaspoon chili powder
3 cups leftover mashed potatoes
4 eggs, separated
1 tablespoon chopped parsley

Heat oven to 350°F. Partially fry bacon in a skillet, saving the drippings. Heat milk in a saucepan; add cheese, stirring thoroughly until cheese is melted. Add bacon drippings, Worcestershire sauce, Tabasco, and chili powder. Combine milk mixture with mashed potatoes and blend. Add egg yolks and beat well. Beat egg whites until stiff but not dry. Fold into potato mixture. Turn into an ungreased 2-quart baking dish and top with bacon strips. Bake 45 to 50 minutes. Sprinkle with parsley. Makes 6 servings.

Sweet Potato Casserole Delight

2 cups mashed leftover sweet
  potatoes
2 tablespoons butter, melted
2 tablespoons flour
½ cup grated Swiss cheese
½ cup grated Parmesan cheese

½ cup milk
¼ cup light cream
3 eggs, separated
½ teaspoon salt
¼ teaspoon nutmeg
dash mace

Heat oven to 375°F. Combine sweet potatoes, butter, flour, cheeses, milk, and cream; blend well. Beat in egg yolks, one at a time. Season with salt, nutmeg, and mace. Beat egg whites until stiff but not dry. Fold into sweet potato mixture. Turn into a buttered 1-quart baking dish. Bake 45 minutes or until puffed and lightly browned. Makes 6 servings.

Pomme de Terre Provençale

8 slices bacon, diced	¼ teaspoon pepper
½ cup diced green pepper	6 eggs
½ cup finely chopped green onion	¼ cup heavy cream
1½ cups diced cooked potato	¼ cup milk
½ teaspoon salt	paprika

Fry bacon in a large, heavy skillet until browned. Remove and set aside. Pour off all but 3 tablespoons drippings. Add green pepper and onion; cook 5 minutes. Add potato; cook until lightly browned, stirring occasionally. Season with salt and pepper. Beat eggs with cream and milk just enough to mix. Pour egg mixture carefully into the pan over the vegetables. Cook over low heat, stirring lightly, until eggs are set but still moist and creamy. Sprinkle with paprika and reserved bacon and serve immediately. Makes 4 servings.

Gnocchi di Brindisi

This Italian specialty is an international dish.

1 cup flour	1 cup grated Parmesan cheese
2 cups mashed potatoes	2 cups Mornay Sauce (*see below*)
2 tablespoons butter	½ cup grated Gruyère cheese
1 egg, beaten with 1 egg yolk	1 tablespoon minced parsley
dash nutmeg	

Sprinkle a wooden board or flat surface generously with some of the flour. Place potatoes on board. With a fork, quickly work in butter, egg, ¾ cup of the flour, and nutmeg. Knead mixture lightly with remaining flour and ½ cup of the Parmesan cheese, until dough is smooth and pliable. Cut off egg-size knobs of dough; roll into finger-sized rolls. Cut in 1-inch pieces. With the back of a floured fork, press in lightly and roll fork forward to simulate shell indentation. Place prepared dough on a towel and let stand 1 hour. Drop gnocchi, a few at a time, into a large, heavy kettle of boiling salted water. Cook gently 4 to 6 minutes or until light and slightly puffed. Remove with a slotted spoon. Continue until all are cooked. Heat oven to 400°F.

Layer drained, cooked gnocchi in a buttered, shallow 2-quart baking dish with Mornay Sauce and the remaining ½ cup Parmesan cheese in between. Sprinkle Gruyère cheese and parsley on top. Bake 15 to 20 minutes or until bubbly hot and browned on top. Makes 8 servings.

Mornay Sauce

2 tablespoons butter
3 tablespoons flour
2 cups milk, scalded
½ teaspoon salt

⅛ teaspoon pepper
dash cayenne
2 tablespoons grated Swiss cheese

Melt butter in a medium saucepan; blend in flour. Stir over low heat 2 minutes. Do not allow to brown. Gradually stir in scalded milk. Cook over moderate heat, stirring constantly, until mixture comes to a boil. Season with salt, pepper, and cayenne. Blend in Swiss cheese. Makes about 2 cups.

Prospector's Soufflé

¾ teaspoon salt
dash pepper
4 eggs, separated
1½ cups cooked vegetables, drained, chopped
1 tablespoon chopped parsley

1 tablespoon chopped celery
2 tablespoons minced onion
3 tablespoons grated Parmesan cheese
1 teaspoon mixed herbs
2 tablespoons vegetable oil

Add salt and pepper to egg yolks and beat until thick. Fold in vegetables, parsley, celery, onion, cheese, and herbs. Heat oven to 350°F. Beat egg whites until stiff. Fold into vegetable mixture. Heat vegetable oil in a large, heavy skillet until hot. Pour in mixture; bake 20 minutes. Makes 4 servings.

Beets à l'Orange

¼ cup orange juice
½ teaspoon grated orange rind
1 tablespoon lemon juice
2 tablespoons sugar

1½ teaspoons cornstarch
¼ teaspoon salt
1½ cups cooked beets
1 tablespoon butter

Combine orange juice, rind, and lemon juice in a small saucepan; heat thoroughly. Combine sugar, cornstarch, and salt; add to hot liquid, stirring constantly, until smooth and thickened. Add beets and butter; heat through and serve at once. Makes 4 servings.

Mashed Potatoes Royale

1½ cups mashed potatoes
2 tablespoons butter
1 egg
½ cup light cream, hot

½ teaspoon salt
dash pepper
⅛ teaspoon paprika

Heat oven to 375°F. Combine all ingredients except paprika. Beat well. Turn into a greased 1-quart baking dish. Sprinkle with paprika. Bake until top is lightly browned, about 10 minutes. Makes 4 servings.

Garden Vegetable Ring

1 package lemon-flavored gelatin
1½ cups boiling water
1 tablespoon vinegar
¾ cup shredded cabbage
¼ cup chopped parsley

½ cup diced celery
2 tablespoons chopped green pepper
½ cup cooked peas
½ cup diced cooked carrot
¼ teaspoon salt

Dissolve gelatin in boiling water; cool. Add remaining ingredients. Stir well and turn into a 6-cup ring mold. Chill in refrigerator overnight or until firm. Unmold and serve. Makes 6 servings.

Three-Spice Patties

At our PTA circle we called this our 1-2-3 quick meal.

1 cup leftover mashed potatoes
½ pound ground beef
1 egg
½ teaspoon salt
⅛ teaspoon pepper
¼ teaspoon oregano
⅛ teaspoon thyme

⅛ teaspoon basil
2 tablespoons minced onion
¼ cup dry milk solids
flour
shortening
1 can (10½ ounces) condensed
   tomato soup

Mix potatoes with beef, egg, seasonings, spices, onion, and dry milk solids. Form into 6 patties about 1 inch thick. Coat with flour. Brown patties on both sides in shortening. Add tomato soup; cover and simmer 25 minutes. Makes 6 servings.

SANDWICHES

Suggestions for Sandwich Making

To make sandwich fillings use your imagination and whatever is on hand. Even if the leftover ingredient quantity is small, don't throw it away. Make individual sandwiches and label them with small flags on wooden picks for easy identification and offer several varieties of one-of-a-kind.

Use white, whole wheat, rye, nut, date, pumpernickel, whole-grain dark, cheese, garlic, cracked wheat, or corn bread and almost any type of roll.

Spread soft butter or margarine to the edge on both slices of bread to prevent filling from soaking in. Season filling before spreading.

Lettuce leaves, tomato slices, pickles, and bacon should be added to sandwiches just before serving. Use colorful garnishes to complement the flavor of the filling, such as olives, pickles, celery sticks, radishes, carrot sticks, pickled onions, tiny cherry tomatoes, green pepper cut into thin strips, and thinly sliced cucumbers.

Sandwich Fillings

Cheese

Cream cheese, chopped stuffed olives, and chopped walnuts.

Cream cheese, drained crushed pineapple, and chopped almonds.

Cream cheese, Roquefort cheese, crumbled bacon, and chopped pecans.

Cream cheese, apricot juice, and mayonnaise.

Cream cheese, finely shredded cucumber, minced onion tops.

Cream cheese, dried beef pieces, grated onion, and diced celery.

Cottage cheese, minced green pepper, chopped parsley, and minced onion.

Roquefort cheese, chopped chicken, and crumbled bacon.

Blue cheese, finely chopped almonds, and grated onion.

Shredded American cheese, chopped pimiento, onion, pickle, hard-cooked eggs, and mayonnaise.

Shredded American cheese, bacon pieces, chopped pickles, olives, Worcestershire sauce, and mayonnaise.

Cottage cheese, bacon pieces, horseradish, salt, pepper, and mayonnaise.

Eggs

Chopped hard-cooked egg, chopped ham, minced green pepper, and green onion with salad dressing.

Chopped hard-cooked egg, pickle relish, pimiento, and mayonnaise.

Chopped hard-cooked egg, chopped stuffed olives, chopped celery, salt, pepper, and mayonnaise.

Chopped hard-cooked egg, finely minced celery, onion, parsley, green pepper, crumbled crisp bacon, salt and pepper, and mayonnaise.

Chopped hard-cooked egg, deviled ham, Worcestershire sauce, and chopped pickle.

Chopped hard-cooked egg, chopped onion, pickle, and crumbled crisp bacon.

Chopped hard-cooked egg, crumbled bacon, drained pickle relish, finely chopped radish, carrot, with mayonnaise.

Fish

Flaked salmon, chopped celery, sweet pickle, and mayonnaise.

Crabmeat, chopped celery, parsley, dash of lemon juice, and mayonnaise.

Chopped cooked lobster meat, chopped mushrooms, green pepper, curry powder, Worcestershire sauce, and mayonnaise.

Red caviar, chopped cucumber (drained), riced hard-cooked egg, onion juice, and salad dressing.

Flaked tuna fish, chopped celery, egg, pimiento, sweet pickle, salt, pepper, and mayonnaise.

Minced cooked shrimp, onion, lemon juice, salt, and mayonnaise.

Minced tuna, horseradish, cream cheese, lemon juice, and mayonnaise.

Chopped cooked lobster, minced onion, diced celery, lemon juice, salt, paprika, and salad dressing.

Meat

Leftover ground roast beef, chopped pickle and celery, horseradish, and mayonnaise.

Chopped corned beef, grated onion, chopped kosher pickle, celery, parsley, and tomato purée.

Chopped cooked beef, chili sauce, minced celery, water cress, salt, pepper, and prepared mustard.

Mashed leftover baked beans with chopped frankfurter, minced onion, prepared mustard, and mayonnaise.

Ground cooked chicken, ground blanched almonds, drained pineapple, and mayonnaise.

Ground ham, chopped gherkins, prepared mustard, and mayonnaise.

Chopped almonds, ground cooked ham, hard-cooked egg, horseradish, and mayonnaise.

Ground cooked ham, minced green pepper, prepared mustard, minced onion, and mayonnaise.

Chopped cooked ham, chopped celery, chopped red apple, and salad dressing.

MINI-MEALS
FOR TWO

Even the best planner will sometimes be caught with left-overs in such small amounts—a cup of cooked chopped beef, half a cup of fish or chicken—that the temptation is to throw them away. But such small supplies, plus ingenuity, can be the basis of a creditable meal for two.

When a friend or neighbor drops in unexpectedly just at lunchtime, don't let your hospitable instincts be smothered—those oddments in the refrigerator will see you through, as the following recipes will show you.

BEEF

Boeuf à Deux

1 tablespoon chopped onion	1 cup coarsely chopped cooked beef
3 teaspoons butter	1 cup hot mashed potatoes
1½ teaspoons flour	2 tablespoons grated Parmesan
¾ cup consommé	cheese
1½ teaspoons tomato purée	1 tablespoon fine bread crumbs
1 teaspoon chopped parsley	1 tablespoon chopped walnuts
1 teaspoon chopped celery	

Heat oven to 450°F. Sauté onion in 1½ teaspoons of the butter in a medium skillet until lightly browned. Blend in flour gradually; stir and cook 1 minute. Gradually add consommé and tomato purée and continue cooking, stirring constantly, until mixture is smooth and thickened. Stir in parsley and celery. Add beef; stir and bring just to boiling point. Turn into a 1-quart baking dish. Spread potatoes on top. Sprinkle with cheese and bread crumbs. Dot with remaining butter. Sprinkle walnuts on top. Bake 10 minutes or until top is delicately browned.

Tijuana Bake

I recommend this for a hungry twosome.

¾ cup milk
½ cup prepared pancake mix
2 tablespoons butter, melted
1 tablespoon chopped peanuts
1 egg yolk, well beaten
1 tablespoon finely chopped onion
3 tablespoons bacon fat
1 cup finely chopped cooked beef

½ teaspoon salt
⅛ teaspoon pepper
1 tablespoon minced parsley
¼ cup commercial sour cream
1 tablespoon grated Parmesan
  cheese
⅛ teaspoon thyme

Add milk to pancake mix in a medium-sized bowl; stir in 1 tablespoon of the butter, peanuts, and egg yolk. Beat well; let stand. Sauté onion in 1 tablespoon of the bacon fat. Stir in beef; cook 2 minutes. Season with salt and pepper and add to pancake batter. Warm the oven. Cook pancakes in remaining bacon fat, one at a time, in a heavy 6-inch skillet. Sprinkle each cooked pancake with parsley; roll each up, and lay in a shallow, well-greased 1½-quart baking dish, packing pancakes close together. Keep baking dish in warmed oven until all pancake batter is used up. Heat oven to 350°F. Brush pancake rolls with the remaining butter and the sour cream and sprinkle with Parmesan cheese. Sprinkle thyme over all. Bake 10 minutes or until cheese is melted. Place under broiler a moment to lightly brown top.

Pierrot Beef with Rice

The sauce makes this dish interesting.

1½ tablespoons butter
1½ teaspoons chopped green
  pepper
1½ teaspoons chopped onion
1 teaspoon chopped celery
1½ tablespoons flour
¾ cup consommé
¼ cup tomato purée
1 cup coarsely chopped cooked beef

½ teaspoon salt
⅛ teaspoon pepper
⅛ teaspoon paprika
dash Tabasco
½ teaspoon lemon juice
¼ teaspoon prepared horseradish,
  drained
fluffy hot rice

Melt butter in a medium skillet and sauté green pepper, onion, and celery until soft but not brown. Blend in flour. Gradually stir in consommé and tomato purée. Add beef; season with salt, pepper, paprika, and Tabasco. Stir in lemon juice and horseradish. Heat thoroughly. Serve on fluffy hot rice.

Caliente Corn Pie

A Mexican version toned down for mild palates.

2 strips bacon
1 cup coarsely ground cooked beef
1 small onion, sliced
¼ cup seedless raisins
¼ cup sliced stuffed olives
1 tablespoon chopped pimiento

½ cup cooked corn
½ teaspoon salt
⅛ teaspoon pepper
1 tablespoon chopped parsley
1½ teaspoons butter

Heat oven to 350°F. Sauté bacon in a skillet until crisp. Chop up and combine with beef. Discard all but 2 tablespoons bacon fat in the skillet, add onion and sauté until lightly brown. Add meat mixture and sauté over high heat until lightly browned. In a 1-quart baking dish place alternate layers of meat mixture and combined raisins, olives, and pimiento. Spread corn on top. Season with salt and pepper. Sprinkle with parsley; dot with butter. Bake 20 minutes.

Brazilian Beef Chili

I especially liked the contrast in texture and flavor of this Rio de Janeiro delicacy.

1 small onion, finely chopped
1 small green pepper, finely
    chopped
1 tablespoon margarine
1 cup canned tomatoes
2 tablespoons tomato paste
1 teaspoon chili powder

½ teaspoon salt
⅛ teaspoon pepper
¼ teaspoon paprika
1 teaspoon Worcestershire sauce
1 cup coarsely ground cooked beef
1 cup cooked kidney beans
1 cup cooked spaghetti

Brown onion and green pepper in margarine in a heavy skillet. Add tomatoes, tomato paste, and seasonings. Cover; simmer gently 40 minutes, stirring frequently. Add beef; continue cooking 15 minutes. Add kidney beans and spaghetti just before serving; heat thoroughly and serve at once.

Duo Roast Beef Hash

1 cup coarsely chopped cooked beef
¾ cup diced cooked potatoes
1 medium onion, chopped
½ teaspoon salt

⅛ teaspoon pepper
3 tablespoons leftover beef gravy
1 tablespoon bacon fat
parsley sprigs

Combine beef, potatoes, onion, salt, and pepper with enough gravy to moisten thoroughly. Heat bacon fat in a heavy 8-inch skillet. Turn in the hash
and stir well; cover and cook over low heat until underside is browned. Fold
over and slide onto a heated serving platter. Garnish with parsley sprigs.

Tongue Hash Marguerite

1 cup coarsely chopped cooked tongue	1 teaspoon minced celery
1 cup coarsely chopped cooked potatoes	2 to 4 tablespoons tongue broth
¼ cup minced onion	¼ teaspoon marjoram
1 teaspoon minced parsley	dash thyme
	½ teaspoon salt
	⅛ teaspoon pepper

Combine tongue, potatoes, onion, parsley, and celery in a medium, heavy
skillet. Pour over enough broth in which tongue was boiled to moisten
through. Cook over medium heat 5 minutes. Add marjoram, thyme, salt,
and pepper and blend in. Cover; reduce heat and simmer 20 minutes or
until thoroughly hot. Serve at once.

LAMB

Lamb Africaine

The original African recipe called for a "grass" lamb, which meant the
young animal had grazed one season.

1 small onion, chopped	¼ teaspoon chervil
½ clove garlic, mashed	¼ teaspoon basil
1 tablespoon olive oil	⅛ teaspoon marjoram
1 small eggplant, peeled, cut in 1-inch cubes	½ teaspoon salt
½ cup canned tomatoes	¼ teaspoon pepper
1 teaspoon tomato paste	1 cup coarsely chopped cooked lamb
1 small bay leaf	1 cup hot fluffy rice

Sauté onion and garlic in olive oil in a medium, heavy skillet. Add eggplant;
cook 5 minutes, stirring frequently. Add tomatoes, tomato paste, bay leaf,
herbs, salt, and pepper. Cover; simmer 12 minutes or until eggplant is soft.
Stir in lamb and heat thoroughly. Serve over hot fluffy rice.

Lamburgers De Luxe

1 cup finely chopped cooked lamb
2 tablespoons finely chopped
   green pepper
1 small onion, finely chopped
¼ cup chopped mushrooms
¼ cup chopped celery
1 pullet egg or 1 egg yolk
1 tablespoon butter, melted
1½ tablespoons sour cream

1 tablespoon fine bread crumbs
½ teaspoon salt
⅛ teaspoon pepper
¼ teaspoon paprika
½ teaspoon prepared mustard
1 teaspoon Worcestershire sauce
dash Tabasco
1 tablespoon bacon fat

Combine lamb, pepper, onion, mushrooms, celery, egg or yolk, butter, sour cream, bread crumbs, salt, pepper, paprika, mustard, Worcestershire sauce and Tabasco. Mix vigorously until well blended. Shape into small cakes. Chill 3 hours or until firm. Brown slowly in heated bacon fat in a heavy skillet.

Quickie Lamb Curry

An interesting quick dish with a touch of East Indian flavor.

½ cup sliced mushrooms
½ cup diced apple
3 tablespoons finely chopped onion
1½ tablespoons butter
1 teaspoon curry powder

1¼ cups condensed cream of
   celery soup
1½ cups cubed cooked lamb
1½ cups hot cooked rice
2 tablespoons shredded coconut

Sauté mushrooms, apple, and onion in butter 6 minutes or until soft. Add curry powder, soup, and lamb; simmer 15 minutes. Heap curried lamb on hot rice; sprinkle with coconut and serve.

Near Eastern Lamb Dolmas

In Turkey and Greece this is almost daily fare in the back country.

2 medium onions
¾ cup finely chopped cooked lamb
½ cup cooked rice
1 tablespoon butter, melted
1 teaspoon minced parsley
¼ cup pine nuts

¼ teaspoon salt
⅛ teaspoon pepper
⅛ teaspoon paprika
1 tablespoon ketchup
¾ cup consommé

Heat oven to 350°F. Cut the outer rings of the onions halfway down in four places, so that the centers can be removed easily. Place onions in saucepan; cover with water and cook until just tender. Drain. Place onions in a 1-quart baking dish. Combine lamb with rice, butter, parsley, pine nuts, salt, pepper, and paprika; mix well. Remove centers of boiled onions. Heap lamb mixture into onions; place onion centers on top. Mix ketchup and consommé; pour over lamb mixture. Bake 20 minutes.

Lamb Puffs Grillier

leftover lamb gravy
1 cup chopped cooked lamb
1 small egg, well beaten
1 cup hot mashed potatoes
½ teaspoon salt

⅛ teaspoon pepper
⅛ teaspoon paprika
flour
melted butter

Heat oven to 400°F. Add enough gravy to lamb to make it spreadable. Blend egg, mashed potatoes, salt, pepper, paprika, and enough flour to make a mixture stiff enough to roll out on a floured board. Roll ¼ inch thick; cut with large biscuit cutter. Drop a spoonful of lamb mixture into center of each round; bring up edges to form a three-cornered puff. Press edges together and brush with melted butter. Place puffs on a greased baking sheet; bake 10 to 12 minutes or until browned. Serve with more heated leftover gravy.

Lamb Armentiere

¼ cup rice
1 cup diced cooked lamb
1 small onion, chopped
¼ cup minced celery
½ cup minced green pepper
½ clove garlic, minced
1½ tablespoons vegetable oil

1 cup canned tomatoes
¼ teaspoon salt
dash pepper
2 dashes red hot sauce
⅛ teaspoon mace
⅛ teaspoon nutmeg

Cook rice in salted boiling water 15 minutes or until not quite done. Drain. Combine with lamb. Sauté onion, celery, green pepper, and garlic in vegetable oil in a medium skillet 5 minutes. Add tomatoes and meat mixture and mix well. Season with salt and pepper. Sprinkle with red hot sauce and spices. Heat oven to 350°F. Pour mixture in a 1-quart baking dish. Bake 15 minutes.

Lamb Espagnole

½ cup uncooked rice
2 tablespoons bacon drippings
1 small onion, chopped
½ cup diced celery
1 tablespoon chopped parsley

1 cup canned tomatoes
½ cup water
½ teaspoon salt
⅛ teaspoon pepper
1 cup cooked lamb, in small cubes

Brown rice lightly in bacon drippings, stirring frequently. Add onion, celery, and parsley; cook 5 minutes longer. Add tomatoes, water, salt, and pepper. Cook, covered, over low heat, stirring occasionally, until rice is tender, 20 to 25 minutes. Add lamb. Heat through but do not boil.

Italian Lamb Hash

A zingy, flavorful dish I had in Frascati.

½ cup diced eggplant
2 tablespoons olive oil
¼ cup minced onion
2 tablespoons coarsely chopped green pepper
½ clove garlic, minced
1 cup canned tomatoes, drained
¼ cup leftover gravy

¾ teaspoon salt
⅛ teaspoon pepper
pinch thyme
pinch rosemary
¾ cup diced cooked lamb
½ cup hot cooked rice
1 tablespoon butter
½ teaspoon grated lemon rind

Sauté eggplant slowly in olive oil until tender, about 6 minutes. Remove from pan; drain off excess oil. Add to the pan onion, green pepper, and garlic; sauté until onion is golden. Add tomatoes and gravy. Season with salt, pepper, thyme, and rosemary. Cover; simmer 10 minutes. Add lamb. Mix well; cover and cook 10 minutes longer. Combine rice with butter and lemon rind. Serve with hash.

VEAL

Veal Soufflé de Bramand

1 tablespoon butter	dash nutmeg
1 tablespoon flour	¼ cup soft bread crumbs
½ cup milk	1 cup ground cooked veal
½ cup light cream	1 teaspoon minced onion
½ teaspoon salt	3 eggs, separated
⅛ teaspoon pepper	

Heat oven to 350°F. Melt butter in a medium skillet; remove from heat and blend in flour until smooth. Return to heat; add milk and cream and cook and stir until thickened. Season with salt, pepper, and nutmeg. Add bread crumbs; stir well. Remove from heat. Stir in veal, onion, and slightly beaten egg yolks; cool. Beat egg whites until stiff. Gently fold into meat mixture. Pour into a buttered 4-cup soufflé dish; set in pan of hot water. Bake 45 minutes or until set.

Veal Mont Blanc

A hearty meal for two which originated in the provinces of France.

2 cups diced cooked veal	2 cloves
3 small onions	1 small bay leaf, crushed
1 stalk celery, cut up	3 cups consommé
2 carrots, cut into 1-inch pieces	½ teaspoon salt
2 medium potatoes, pared, quartered	dash pepper
	2 tablespoons flour
1 teaspoon chopped parsley	Baking Powder Biscuit Dough
1 teaspoon chopped celery	(page 154)
½ small clove garlic, minced	

Heat oven to 350°F. Combine veal, onions, celery, carrots, potatoes, parsley, celery, garlic, cloves, and bay leaf. Add 2½ cups of consommé, salt, and pepper. Make a paste with remaining ½ cup consommé and flour and stir into mixture. Turn into a 1-quart baking dish. Bake, covered, 40 minutes or until vegetables are tender. Remove from oven. Cover top with biscuit dough rolled to ½-inch thickness; slash center for steam to escape. Increase heat to 425°F. Bake 12 to 15 minutes.

Veal Rosalinde

½ cup dry red wine
½ teaspoon salt
⅛ teaspoon basil
⅛ teaspoon thyme
½ teaspoon monosodium glutamate
1 veal steak, ¾ inch thick
1½ tablespoons butter

1 can (5 ounces) water chestnuts,
   with liquid
1 can (3 ounces) sliced mushrooms,
   with liquid
2 tablespoons flour
⅛ teaspoon paprika

Combine wine, salt, basil, thyme, and monosodium glutamate. Place meat in a shallow pan; pour in wine mixture and marinate 3 hours. Drain; reserve marinade. Brown meat in butter on both sides. Add marinade; cover, simmer 35 to 40 minutes or until meat is tender. Drain water chestnuts and mushrooms and combine liquid with flour. Stir into pan. Add water chestnuts and mushrooms. Sprinkle with paprika. Heat through.

Aloha Veal Patties

1 cup ground cooked veal
2 tablespoons fine dry bread crumbs
2 tablespoons ketchup
2 tablespoons minced onion
¼ teaspoon salt
dash pepper
⅛ teaspoon marjoram

⅛ teaspoon rosemary
1 egg, slightly beaten
2 slices canned pineapple
1½ tablespoons butter, melted
3 tablespoons brown sugar
¼ cup pineapple syrup

Heat even to 350°F. Combine meat, bread crumbs, ketchup, onion, seasonings, and egg; mix well. Shape into two large patties. Place on pineapple slices in a greased shallow pan. Combine remaining ingredients and spoon over patties; cover. Bake 30 minutes. Uncover; bake 10 minutes longer, basting occasionally.

Marseilles Veal Croquettes

1 tablespoon butter
2 tablespoons flour
¼ cup milk
¼ cup light cream
1 cup ground cooked veal
1 teaspoon salt

1 tablespoon chopped onion
2 tablespoons shredded Cheddar
   cheese
¾ cup fine cracker crumbs
shortening for frying

Melt butter in a medium saucepan. Add flour and stir until blended. Add milk and cream and cook, stirring, to make a smooth, thick white sauce. Add veal, salt, onion, and cheese. Cool. Shape into 4 croquettes. Roll in cracker crumbs. Fry croquettes in hot shortening until well browned. Drain on absorbent paper. Makes 2 servings.

Veal in Wine

1½ cups cubed cooked veal	1 small clove garlic, peeled
2 tablespoons butter	3 medium carrots, pared, diced
⅛ teaspoon marjoram	½ cup white wine
⅛ teaspoon thyme	

Brown veal in butter in a small skillet with marjoram, thyme, and garlic. Discard garlic. Add carrots. Pour wine over all. Cover; simmer 10 minutes.

Veal Italiano

An American adaptation of an Italian favorite.

4 thin slices cooked veal	3 tablespoons shortening
½ cup cracker crumbs	1 can (8 ounces) tomato sauce, heated
½ teaspoon salt	
⅛ teaspoon pepper	¼ pound Mozzarella cheese, thinly sliced
1 small egg, beaten	

Dip veal slices in mixture of crumbs, salt, and pepper, then in egg, and again in crumbs. Brown slices quickly on both sides in hot shortening. Place in a heatproof serving dish. Pour hot tomato sauce over them. Top with cheese. Broil 3 minutes or until cheese melts and is slightly browned.

Golden Acorn Squash

This well-known veal dish is served in many tavernas of Greece.

1 medium acorn squash	6 tablespoons light cream
¾ teaspoon salt	¾ cup finely chopped cooked veal
⅛ teaspoon pepper	½ teaspoon minced parsley
2 teaspoons butter	½ cup buttered bread crumbs
2 teaspoons flour	

Heat oven to 375°F. Cut squash crosswise; scoop out seeds and membrane. Season with half the salt and pepper. Turn upside down on a greased baking sheet; bake 30 to 35 minutes or until just tender, turning them right side up after 15 minutes. Combine butter and flour and make a smooth paste. Heat in a saucepan over medium heat, stir in cream and cook, stirring, until mixture is smooth and thickened. Season with remaining salt and pepper. Add veal and parsley. Fill cavities of squash to heaping. Cover with bread crumbs. Bake 15 minutes longer.

PORK AND HAM

Pork Chen Yuen

¼ cup chopped onion
1½ tablespoons vegetable oil
¾ cup cooked pork, cut in
   julienne strips
¾ cup chicken broth
¼ cup coarsely chopped celery
¼ cup thinly sliced mushrooms
4 water chestnuts, sliced

¼ cup canned bean sprouts,
   well drained
1 tablespoon cornstarch
⅛ teaspoon salt
⅛ teaspoon sugar
¾ tablespoon soy sauce
1 tablespoon water
1 cup Chinese noodles, crisped

Sauté onion in vegetable oil in a medium skillet until soft but not brown. Add pork, chicken broth, celery, mushrooms, bean sprouts, and water chestnuts. Cover; simmer 6 minutes. Combine cornstarch with salt, sugar, soy sauce, and water; stir into a smooth paste. Add to pork mixture, stirring constantly until smooth and thickened. Serve over Chinese noodles.

Savoury Pork Pie

When you're back to two after your family has grown, this is an ideal way to serve leftover meat.

1 package instant pie crust mix
1 cup coarsely chopped cooked
   pork
1 cup diced cooked potatoes
¼ cup cooked green peas
¼ cup cooked green beans
1 teaspoon minced parsley

dash ground cloves
dash nutmeg
¼ cup chopped onions, sautéed
1 tablespoon chopped mushrooms,
   sautéed
¼ cup water
1 teaspoon milk

Heat oven to 400°F. Prepare pie crust mix according to package directions; roll to ⅛-inch thickness. Line a 2-cup baking dish with pie crust, reserving enough for a top crust. Combine remaining ingredients, except milk. Fill baking dish with the mixture. Cover with top crust; slash center. Pinch edges of crust together; brush top with milk. Bake 40 to 45 minutes.

Ham Casserole Parma

This is an Italian favorite which usually calls for veal, but is just as delicous made with ham.

1 cup spinach noodles	½ teaspoon salt
½ cup commercial sour cream	⅛ teaspoon pepper
¼ cup heavy cream	¼ teaspoon paprika
¾ cup grated Swiss cheese	1½ teaspoons butter
1 cup coarsely chopped cooked ham	1 tablespoon chopped parsley

Heat oven to 375°F. Cook noodles in salted boiling water 8 minutes or until just tender. Combine sour cream with heavy cream; heat in medium saucepan to just below boiling. Stir in half of the cheese and all the ham. Season with salt, pepper, and paprika. In a well-greased 1-quart baking dish alternate layers of noodles and ham mixture. Top with remaining cheese; dot with butter. Sprinkle with parsley. Bake 20 to 25 minutes or until top is lightly browned.

Amsterdam Soufflé

2 tablespoons butter	½ cup thinly sliced sautéed mushrooms
1½ tablespoons flour	
½ cup milk	½ teaspoon curry powder
½ cup light cream	pinch of mace
¼ cup grated processed American cheese	¾ teaspoon grated onion
	2 eggs, separated
¼ cup minced celery	½ teaspoon salt
1 tablespoon minced pimiento	⅛ teaspoon pepper
½ cup finely chopped cooked ham	½ teaspoon paprika

Heat oven to 350°F. Melt butter in a medium skillet; stir in flour and the milk and cream gradually, stirring constantly until smooth and thickened. Add cheese; stir until melted. Add celery, pimiento, ham, mushrooms, curry powder, mace, and onion. Beat the egg yolks and stir them in. Season with salt, pepper, and paprika. Cool to lukewarm. Beat egg whites until stiff but not dry; carefully fold into the mixture. Turn into a well-greased 4-cup baking dish. Bake 30 to 35 minutes or until a knife inserted in the center comes out clean.

Quickie Ham Brunch

1 cup minced cooked ham
1 hard-cooked egg, finely chopped
½ cup undiluted cream of
   mushroom soup
¼ teaspoon salt

dash pepper
1 tablespoon bacon fat
Parsley Rice Ring (page 150),
   ½ recipe

Combine ham, egg, soup, salt, and pepper. Chill 3 hours or until mixture holds its shape when formed into patties. Heat bacon fat in a skillet to sizzling point. Brown patties well on both sides. Serve at once with rice. Makes 2 servings.

Pennywise Ham Casserole

½ cup cooked macaroni
½ cup finely chopped cooked ham
1 tablespoon minced celery
1 tablespoon minced green pepper
¼ teaspoon prepared mustard

1 teaspoon minced onion
½ cup milk
¼ cup heavy cream
1 egg, lightly beaten

Heat oven to 350°F. Turn macaroni into the bottom of a greased 1-quart baking dish. Combine ham with celery, green pepper, mustard, and onion and mix well. Spread over macaroni. Combine milk, cream, and egg. Pour over macaroni mixture. Bake 30 minutes or until firm.

Green Peppers California

2 medium green peppers
1 tablespoon butter
1 tablespoon chopped onion
1 tablespoon chopped celery
1 teaspoon flour
¼ cup milk
1 cup ground cooked ham

¾ cup cooked rice
½ teaspoon salt
⅛ teaspoon pepper
2 tablespoons grated Parmesan
   cheese
2 tablespoons water

Split peppers lengthwise; remove seeds and membrane. Parboil 3 minutes in boiling salted water. Drain peppers; carefully turn them upside down and let stand. Heat oven to 400°F. Melt butter in a medium, heavy skillet; add onion and celery and sauté until soft but not brown. Blend in flour. Gradually add milk, stirring constantly, until mixture is smooth and thickened. Stir in ham, rice, salt, and pepper. Lay pepper halves in a greased, shallow 1-quart baking dish and fill them solidly with ham mixture. Sprinkle cheese over the tops. Add water to baking dish. Bake 20 to 25 minutes.

Ham Balinese

2 medium sweet potatoes, cooked
½ cup sliced mushrooms
1½ tablespoons butter
1½ tablespoons flour
1 cup consommé
1¼ cups cubed cooked ham
¾ cup chopped cooked cabbage

1 tablespoon brown sugar
dash allspice
dash nutmeg
¼ cup light cream
2 teaspoons Angostura bitters
1 tablespoon toasted slivered almonds

Heat oven to 350°F. Peel sweet potatoes; set aside. Sauté mushrooms in butter 3 minutes. Blend in flour. Gradually add consommé, stirring constantly, until mixture is smooth and thickened. Place ham and cabbage in a 1-quart baking dish; pour mushroom sauce over. Cover; bake 10 minutes. Mash sweet potatoes, add brown sugar, allspice, and nutmeg. Blend in cream; whip potatoes until light and fluffy. Remove baking dish from oven. Increase heat to 425°F. Stir Angostura bitters into ham mixture. Spread potatoes over the top. Sprinkle with almonds. Bake 25 minutes.

Hot Dog Special

Sherry with hot dogs? Why not—try it and you'll agree they're very compatible.

1½ teaspoons butter
1 small onion, chopped
1 tablespoon chopped green pepper
1 tablespoon chopped celery
1 teaspoon paprika
1 small tomato, peeled and sliced

2 cooked frankfurters, cut in ½-inch pieces
2 tablespoons sherry
¾ teaspoon salt
⅛ teaspoon pepper
2 eggs, well beaten

Melt butter in a heavy, medium-sized skillet; add onion, green pepper, and celery and lightly sauté until soft. Add paprika and frankfurters; sauté over very low heat 5 minutes. Add tomato and wine. Season with salt and pepper. Cover and simmer gently 12 to 15 minutes. Pour in eggs; stir gently, and cook over low heat until eggs are just set.

Lumberman's Soup

1½ teaspoons margarine	1 cup leftover baked beans
1 small onion, sliced	1 small stalk celery, cut up
½ clove garlic, minced	½ teaspoon chopped parsley
3 tablespoons chopped green pepper	⅛ teaspoon marjoram
½ cup peeled, chopped tomato	⅛ teaspoon rosemary
1 cup consommé	½ teaspoon salt
2 cooked frankfurters, coarsely chopped	⅛ teaspoon pepper
	2 tablespoons sherry

Melt margarine in a small heavy pan; add onion, garlic, and pepper and sauté until tender but not brown. Add tomato, consommé, frankfurters, beans, celery, parsley, marjoram, rosemary, salt, and pepper. Bring to a boil; reduce heat and simmer 30 minutes. Stir in sherry and serve.

CHICKEN

Chicken Soufflé Nakka

In a small Swedish town called Nakka, I was served a dish similar to this.

1 tablespoon minced onion	1 tablespoon finely chopped mushrooms
2 tablespoons butter	2 tablespoons fine bread crumbs
2 tablespoons flour	1 egg yolk, slightly beaten
½ cup light cream	½ teaspoon chervil
½ cup chicken broth	½ teaspoon minced parsley
½ teaspoon salt	½ teaspoon minced celery
⅛ teaspoon pepper	½ teaspoon chopped chives
1 cup finely chopped cooked chicken	2 egg whites, beaten stiff
2 tablespoons blanched, shredded, toasted almonds	dash nutmeg

Heat oven to 400°F. Sauté onion in butter until soft but not brown. Stir in flour until smooth. Stir in cream and broth. Cook over low heat, stirring constantly, until sauce is smooth and thickened. Season with salt and pepper. Add chicken, almonds, mushrooms, bread crumbs, egg yolk, chervil, parsley, celery, and chives. Fold in egg whites and nutmeg. Pour into a well-greased casserole. Bake 30 to 35 minutes or until a knife inserted in the center comes out clean.

Chicken à la King Rogano

This is Roman style and a family specialty.

1 tablespoon butter	1 cup light cream
½ cup thinly sliced mushrooms	½ cup chicken broth
1 small green pepper, thinly sliced	¾ teaspoon salt
¼ cup drained, sliced, canned pimiento	¼ teaspoon white pepper
	2 egg yolks
1 cup diced cooked chicken	pinch of nutmeg
2 tablespoons margarine	2 baked patty shells
2 tablespoons flour	2 sprigs of parsley

Heat butter in a heavy skillet; add mushrooms and green pepper and sauté until tender, about 6 minutes. Add pimiento and chicken; heat 3 minutes. Remove from heat. Combine margarine and flour in a medium saucepan and stir to a smooth paste. Slowly add cream and chicken broth and cook over low heat, stirring constantly, until mixture is smooth and thickened. Season with salt and pepper. Beat in egg yolks one at a time. Stir in nutmeg. Add chicken mixture. Reheat thoroughly. Serve in patty shells; garnish with parsley.

Chicken Omelet Marvella

Intimate and grand—for two, of course.

6 tablespoons milk	¼ cup chopped black olives
½ cup diced cooked chicken	4 eggs, beaten
½ can (10½ ounces) condensed cream of chicken soup	¼ teaspoon salt
	¼ teaspoon white pepper
½ teaspoon Worcestershire sauce	1 tablespoon butter
dash Tabasco	1 tablespoon chopped parsley

Heat 3 tablespoons of the milk with the chicken, cream of chicken soup, Worcestershire sauce, Tabasco, and olives. Combine eggs with remaining milk, salt, and pepper. Heat butter in a medium, heavy skillet and pour in egg mixture. Cook, lifting edges with a spatula to allow uncooked egg to run under. When omelet is done, cover half with some of the hot chicken mixture; fold over and slide onto a heated platter. Top with remaining chicken mixture. Sprinkle with parsley and serve immediately.

Chicken Croquettes Maupassant

Every tourist to France should remember this.

½ cup chicken broth
1½ teaspoons butter
1 teaspoon flour
1 cup finely chopped cooked chicken
2 tablespoons chopped pistachio nuts
½ teaspoon lemon juice
½ teaspoon minced onion

1 teaspoon minced parsley
½ teaspoon minced celery
½ teaspoon chili powder
2 eggs
fine bread crumbs
shortening for frying
Mushroom Sauce (page 112),
    ½ recipe

Heat chicken broth in a saucepan. Combine butter and flour to make a paste. Add to hot broth; stir constantly until mixture is smooth and thickened. Cook 4 minutes over low heat. Stir in chicken, nuts, lemon juice, onion, parsley, celery, and chili powder. Remove from heat. Beat in 1 egg until well blended. Spread mixture on a cold platter and chill 1 hour. Beat the remaining egg in a small bowl. Mold chilled chicken mixture into four croquettes. Dip each in bread crumbs, then in beaten egg, and again in bread crumbs. Chill 3 hours. When ready to serve, fry croquettes in deep fat at 390°F. until golden brown all over. Drain on absorbent paper. Serve with Mushroom Sauce.

Kobe Chicken and Rice

1 clove garlic, cut in half
1 tablespoon butter, melted
1 tablespoon flour
½ cup chicken broth
¾ teaspoon soy sauce
½ teaspoon salt

⅛ teaspoon pepper
1 cup cooked rice
1 cup cubed cooked chicken
1 tablespoon chopped toasted almonds

Rub a heatproof casserole all over inside with cut garlic; discard garlic. Pour in the butter and blend in flour and chicken broth. Heat over low heat, stirring, until mixture is smooth and thick. Add soy sauce, salt, and pepper. Combine rice and chicken and add to casserole. Sprinkle almonds on top. Cover tightly; cook over very low heat 6. to 8 minutes or until just heated thoroughly.

Elegant Luncheon Salad

In Yugoslavia they prepare this salad in a special clay salad bowl.

¾ cup diced cooked chicken
½ cup small cauliflower flowerets
1 small tomato, peeled, coarsely
  chopped
½ cup cooked string beans,
  frenched

1 hard-cooked egg
2 tablespoons French dressing
½ teaspoon minced parsley
½ teaspoon chopped chives
1 tablespoon chopped walnuts
water cress or Bibb lettuce leaves

Combine chicken, cauliflower, tomato, and string beans in a salad bowl. Cut egg in two; remove yolk. Chop egg white and add to chicken mixture. Mash yolk and blend into French dressing. Toss salad lightly with dressing. Sprinkle top with parsley, chives, and walnuts. Serve on water cress or Bibb lettuce leaves.

TURKEY

Autumn Turkey Casserole

½ cup turkey gravy
2 tablespoons turkey broth
½ teaspoon tomato sauce
½ teaspoon salt
⅛ teaspoon pepper

⅛ teaspoon paprika
1 cup diced cooked turkey
½ cup cooked green peas
¼ cup sliced mushrooms, sautéed
1 tablespoon buttered bread crumbs

Heat oven to 400°F. Thin gravy with turkey broth. Add tomato sauce, salt, pepper, and paprika. Place half the turkey in a greased 1-quart baking dish. Add the peas and mushrooms to form a layer; layer remaining turkey on top. Pour the sauce over all. Sprinkle with bread crumbs. Bake 20 minutes.

Eliza's Turkey Casserole

The original recipe, which I ate with relish at an English inn, called for partridge.

1 small bunch fresh broccoli, cut into flowerets
1 tablespoon butter
1 tablespoon flour
½ cup milk
½ cup light cream
½ teaspoon salt
¼ teaspoon pepper

½ cup grated Parmesan cheese
1 cup cooked medium-width noodles
1 cup diced cooked turkey
2 tablespoons slivered toasted almonds
½ teaspoon paprika

Cook broccoli in salted boiling water until tender. Heat oven to 350°F. Melt butter in a medium skillet and stir in flour; cook 1 minute. Gradually add milk and cream and cook, stirring constantly, until mixture is smooth and thickened. Season with salt and pepper. Add cheese; simmer over very low heat until cheese is melted, stirring frequently. Spread noodles in the bottom of a 1½-quart baking dish. Arrange turkey over noodles; gently lay broccoli on top. Pour cream sauce over all. Sprinkle with almonds and paprika. Bake 15 minutes or until bubbly.

FISH AND SHELLFISH

Louisiana Fish Creole

2 tablespoons butter
1 tablespoon chopped onion
½ cup chopped celery
1 tablespoon chopped green pepper
2 tablespoons flour
1¼ cups canned tomatoes
2 tablespoons water

1 small bay leaf
½ teaspoon chopped parsley
⅛ teaspoon thyme
1 cup hot fluffy rice
1 cup cooked fish, broken in small pieces

Melt butter in a medium, heavy skillet; add onion, celery, and green pepper and sauté 5 minutes or until almost tender, stirring frequently. Blend in flour. Cook over low heat until slightly brown. Stir in tomatoes and water. Cook, stirring constantly, until thickened. Add remaining ingredients; blend well. Cover and simmer over low heat 10 to 12 minutes.

Leningrad Fish

A Russian inspiration which is universally popular.

2 tablespoons minced onion	1 cup cooked fish, broken in large
1 tablespoon butter	chunks
½ teaspoon paprika	⅛ teaspoon pepper
½ cup commercial sour cream	1½ teaspoons lemon juice
1 egg yolk, lightly beaten	1 cup hot fluffy rice
½ teaspoon salt	1 tablespoon chopped parsley

Sauté onion in butter until lightly browned. Stir in paprika. Add sour cream and heat almost to boiling, stirring constantly. Stir a little of the mixture into the egg yolk; add to remaining cream mixture. Cook over low heat, stirring gently, until slightly thickened. Add salt, fish, and pepper. Heat lemon juice and stir it into the sauce. Serve immediately over hot fluffy rice, with parsley sprinkled on top.

Codfish Jubilee

Lots of protein in this delicious dish.

¼ cup butter	¼ teaspoon Worcestershire
2 tablespoons flour	sauce
¼ teaspoon salt	1 cup milk
⅛ teaspoon pepper	½ cup shredded Cheddar cheese
⅛ teaspoon paprika	1 cup flaked, cooked codfish
dash Tabasco	2 tablespoons soft bread crumbs

Heat oven to 400°F. Melt half the butter in a medium skillet; stir in flour and seasonings, over low heat. Gradually add milk and cook, stirring, until sauce is smooth and thickened. Stir in half the cheese. Place fish in a shallow 1-quart baking dish. Pour sauce over it. Mix remaining cheese with crumbs and sprinkle over mixture. Dot with remaining butter. Bake 20 minutes. Makes 2 servings.

Springtime Salmon Ring

1 cup mashed cooked carrots	2 eggs, well beaten
1 tablespoon butter, melted	½ cup milk
¼ teaspoon salt	¾ cup leftover creamed salmon
dash pepper	1 teaspoon chopped parsley
1 teaspoon minced onion	

Heat oven to 350°F. Combine carrots, butter, salt, pepper, onion, eggs, and milk; mix well. Turn into a well-greased 2-cup ring mold. Set in a pan of hot water; bake 40 minutes or until top is firm to the touch. Let stand 3 minutes. Unmold on heated serving platter. Fill center with hot creamed salmon. Garnish with parsley.

Lobster Finesso Salad

½ cup diced cooked lobster
¼ cup diced heart of celery
¼ cup finely shredded crisp lettuce
1½ tablespoons mayonnaise
1½ teaspoons chili sauce
½ teaspoon ketchup
¼ teaspoon Worcestershire sauce

dash Tabasco
2 tablespoons peeled, finely chopped tomato
¼ teaspoon chopped chives
¼ teaspoon minced parsley
¼ teaspoon salt
crisp lettuce cups

Combine lobster, celery, and lettuce. Chill 30 minutes. Mix mayonnaise, chili sauce, ketchup, Worcestershire sauce, Tabasco, tomato, chives, parsley, and salt. Gently blend with lobster mixture. Heap on lettuce cups.

Chinese Soochow Lobster

A supper entrée that's perfect for a special occasion.

1 tablespoon vegetable oil
6 tablespoons finely chopped onion
2 tablespoons minced celery
¼ cup minced cucumber
2 tablespoons finely chopped mushrooms
¼ cup bean sprouts, cut up
2 water chestnuts, chopped
½ cup chicken broth

1 tablespoon butter
¾ cup finely chopped cooked lobster
2 tablespoons sherry
1 teaspoon flour
½ teaspoon salt
⅛ teaspoon pepper
¾ teaspoon soy sauce
1 cup hot fluffy rice

Heat oil to sizzling point; add onion, celery, cucumber, mushrooms, bean sprouts, and water chestnuts and sauté for 2 minutes, stirring constantly. Add chicken broth; reduce heat. Cover and simmer 4 minutes. Heat half the butter in a small skillet; add lobster meat and sauté 1 minute. Add sherry; simmer 2 minutes. Combine the two mixtures; cook 3 minutes. Make a paste with the remaining butter and the flour; stir into mixture and cook, stirring, until smooth and thickened. Season with salt and pepper. Stir in soy sauce. Serve with rice.

Mariner's Coleslaw

1 cup finely shredded cabbage
3 tablespoons chopped, unpared apple
¼ cup chopped celery
½ cup flaked cooked crabmeat

¼ teaspoon salt
1 tablespoon chili sauce
¼ cup mayonnaise
pinch oregano

Soak cabbage in ice water 30 minutes or until crisp. Drain well and dry on a towel. Blend cabbage with apple, celery, crabmeat, and salt. Combine chili sauce with mayonnaise and oregano. Gently stir into crabmeat mixture.

Seaside Cakes

1 cup flaked cooked crabmeat
½ cup soft bread crumbs
1 egg
½ teaspoon dry mustard
pinch thyme
½ teaspoon salt

⅛ teaspoon pepper
⅛ teaspoon paprika
dash Worcestershire sauce
3 tablespoons flour
shortening for frying
½ cup hot tomato sauce

Combine crabmeat, bread crumbs, egg, mustard, thyme, salt, pepper, paprika, and Worcestershire sauce; blend well. Shape into four small cakes. Roll each in flour; chill 3 hours. When ready to serve, fry to golden brown on both sides in hot fat. Drain on absorbent paper. Serve with tomato sauce.

Shrimp Salad Alexandra

½ cup mayonnaise
¾ teaspoon prepared mustard
dash Worcestershire sauce
2 teaspoons minced sweet gherkins
1 teaspoon chopped capers
1 teaspoon minced parsley
1 teaspoon minced celery
½ teaspoon chervil

½ teaspoon tarragon
¼ teaspoon anchovy paste
½ teaspoon salt
⅛ teaspoon pepper
⅛ teaspoon paprika
1 cup cooked shrimp, halved
crisp lettuce leaves

Combine all ingredients except shrimp and lettuce leaves, beating vigorously to blend well. Add shrimp; mix well. Chill 2 hours. Serve on lettuce leaves.

Oyster Faloush

The inns in Lyons, France, often serve this dish.

½ cup heavy cream
1 tablespoon butter
1 tablespoon flour
¼ teaspoon salt

dash pepper
1 egg, slightly beaten
½ cup cooked oysters
1 teaspoon chopped parsley

Heat cream. Melt butter in a small skillet; stir in flour and cream. Cook, stirring constantly, until thickened. Season with salt and pepper. Stir in egg. Add oysters; simmer 1 minute. Serve immediately on buttered toast, patty shells, leftover hot cooked rice, or buttered noodles, or mix with cooked macaroni. Garnish with chopped parsley.

VEGETABLES

Farmer's Potato Soup

2 tablespoons coarsely chopped
  onion
1 cup mashed potatoes
1½ cups milk
1½ teaspoons butter

½ teaspoon salt
dash white pepper
1 teaspoon chopped chives
¼ teaspoon paprika

Cover onion with water in a medium saucepan; cover and simmer gently until onion is soft and water has evaporated. Stir in mashed potatoes; cook 2 minutes. Heat milk with butter almost to scalding point. Put potato mixture through a food mill or sieve; stir into hot milk. Season with salt and pepper. Heat thoroughly but do not allow to boil. Serve in soup bowls garnished with chives and paprika.

Beer Garden Potato Salad

A good, easy, and thrifty way to use leftover potatoes.

½ teaspoon sugar
¼ teaspoon salt
⅛ teaspoon dry mustard
1 tablespoon mild vinegar
½ cup commercial sour cream

¼ cup thinly sliced cucumber
1 tablespoon minced celery
1 cup sliced boiled potatoes
½ teaspoon paprika

Combine sugar with salt, mustard, and vinegar. Stir into sour cream and blend well. Add cucumber and celery to potatoes. Gently stir in sour cream dressing until potatoes are well coated. Sprinkle with paprika and serve at once.

Touch-Of-Spring Salad

A real pick-me-upper for wilted appetites.

¾ cup cooked lima beans, drained
½ teaspoon minced onion
3 tablespoons French dressing
¼ cup mayonnaise
2 hard-cooked eggs, sliced
½ cup sliced celery

½ teaspoon salt
⅛ teaspoon pepper
crisp lettuce greens
1 teaspoon chopped parsley
paprika

Moisten beans and onion with French dressing. Let stand 20 minutes, then drain. Add mayonnaise, eggs, celery, salt, and pepper. Mix lightly. Chill. Serve on lettuce greens, sprinkled with parsley and paprika.

Southern Sweet Potato Soufflé

Treat someone special to this special dish. It is easy to prepare even for only two servings.

1 cup cooked sweet potatoes
¼ cup hot milk
2 tablespoons brandy, heated
2 tablespoons butter, melted
dash cayenne

⅛ teaspoon nutmeg
½ teaspoon salt
½ teaspoon grated lemon rind
2 eggs, separated

Heat oven to 400°F. Beat potatoes vigorously with milk, brandy, and butter until smooth. Add seasonings. Beat egg yolks thoroughly and blend into potato mixture. Beat egg whites until stiff but not dry. Fold into potato mixture. Turn into a well-greased 1-quart baking dish. Bake 20 minutes or until well puffed and delicately browned.

COOKING
INFORMATION

EVERYDAY LEFTOVER COOKING HINTS

- To freshen French or Italian bread or hard rolls, sprinkle the crust with a few drops of ice water and place bread or rolls in a preheated 350°F. oven for 10 minutes.
- Save leftover sandwiches for snacks and lunches. Brush with mixture of melted butter and lemon juice. Sauté until lightly browned.
- To make cutouts for fancy sandwiches from bread slices, first freeze bread then use cookie cutters for fancy shaping.
- Save the rinds of lemons, oranges, and grapefruits. Grate them and place in tightly covered jars. Store in refrigerator until needed. Use as flavorings in frostings, sauces, and cakes.
- To use leftover ketchup, combine 3 tablespoons oil, 1 tablespoon vinegar, $1/8$ teaspoon each marjoram and paprika with $1/4$ cup or less ketchup; shake bottle well. Makes a delicious salad dressing.
- Use leftover mashed potatoes as a frosting for cupcakes. Beat in confectioners' sugar and vanilla extract until well blended and of spreading consistency.
- Chop leftover dates and mix with apples when baking an apple pie.
- Bake leftover meat loaf or meatball mixture in greased muffin pans for attractive individual servings.
- Ground leftover salami added to ground beef will give an unusual flavor to hamburgers and meat loaf.
- Use chopped toasted almonds as a garnish for fish, or mix with string beans or peas for pleasant crunchiness.
- Use leftover sweet pickle juice instead of vinegar when making dressing for coleslaw.
- Adding a little leftover coffee to a gravy will give it a rich brown color without coffee flavor.
- Stir a little leftover oatmeal into a stew for added flavor and thickening.

- If you have a leftover frankfurter, slice it and brown in butter. Add slices to hot cream of pea soup.
- Store liquid from canned vegetables, mushrooms, etc., in freezer and use in soup stock and gravies.
- For a delicious flavor, add leftover chopped walnuts or pecans to wild rice during last ten minutes of cooking.
- To make croutons, cut stale bread in ½-inch squares and fry in butter until golden brown. Shake skillet or toss with fork. Serve in salads or atop cream soups.
- To make toast cups, cut crusts from thinly sliced stale bread and brush generously with melted butter. Press into large muffin cups. Toast in 350°F. oven 10 to 15 minutes. Fill with creamed vegetable or meat mixture.
- Cut leftover angel food cake into 2-inch square pieces. Gently mold into balls. Dip into a fluffy white frosting. Roll in moist shredded coconut and make Coconut Balls. Tint coconut, if desired.
- For Mock Angel Food—Dip stale bread slices in sweetened condensed milk, then in flaked coconut. Place on baking sheet and toast in hot oven until bread is heated through and coconut is browned.
- Cut thin slices of stale bread into fingers, rounds, or any small shape you wish. Quickly brown in butter on one side only. These may be made ahead of time. Spread canapés topping on untoasted side just before serving.
- For an easy canapé spread mash cooked leftover crabmeat, shrimp, salmon, lobster, or tuna. Moisten with mayonnaise, add a few drops lemon juice and some minced parsley.

To store Whole Raw Egg Yolks
Place yolks in jar with tight-fitting lid. Add water to cover yolks. Refrigerate, covered, until ready to use. Drain before using. Do not keep longer than 3 days.

To store Raw Egg Whites
Refrigerate egg whites in jar wtih tight-fitting lid until ready to use. Egg whites may be kept a week to 10 days.

To Cook Egg Yolks
In small saucepan, bring 3 cups water and ½ teaspoon salt to boiling. Gently slip an egg yolk into boiling water. Reduce heat; simmer, uncovered, 5 minutes or until yolk is firm.

To Use Raw Egg Whites
Beat one egg white with 2 tablespoons sugar until stiff. Fold into hot cooked puddings just until combined. Or use for meringues, in frostings, cakes, etc.

- Roast meat can be cut into julienne strips and marinated in a sharp French dressing. Use in salads or mix with vegetables.
- For an emergency supper dish, use bits and pieces of meat combined with a cooked pasta product, commercial sour cream, crushed bay leaf, chopped green pepper, onion, celery, and mushrooms and heated in the oven.
- Chop leftover vegetables, macaroni, spaghetti, and noodles for mulligatawny soup.
- Make Cornish pies using leftover meat and vegetables.
- Squares of roast meats on a skewer alternated with green pepper strips, small boiled onions, and mushrooms, and brushed with a sharp marinade, make an emergency luncheon treat.
- Fluff and use mashed potatoes as a topping on meat loaf.
- Use leftover mashed potatoes in chocolate cake and cookies.
- Lining a casserole with mashed potatoes and filling it with a stew gives the dish a festive appearance.
- Reheat mashed potatoes in oven with a topping of grated Cheddar cheese and a sprinkling of chopped almonds.
- When fresh vegetables are cooked until just tender, they hold their shape for the second time around.
- Marinate cooked vegetables in French dressing and use in salads.
- Fill omelets with cooked vegetables and baste with a hot chili sauce.
- Add cooked carrots to pancake batter.

TABLE OF SUBSTITUTIONS

1 teaspoon *baking powder*	1 teaspoon cream of tartar plus 1 teaspoon baking soda
1 cup canned *beef bouillon*	1 beef bouillon cube or 1 envelope instant beef broth or 1 teaspoon beef extract dissolved in 1 cup boiling water
1 cup *beef stock*	1 cup canned beef broth
1 cup *buttermilk*	1 cup milk plus 1 tablespoon vinegar
1 cup canned *chicken broth*	1 chicken bouillon cube or 1 envelope instant chicken broth dissolved in 1 cup boiling water
1 cup *chicken stock*	1 cup canned chicken broth
½ cup *chili sauce*	½ cup tomato sauce plus 2 tablespoons sugar, 1 tablespoon vinegar, ⅛ teaspoon ground cloves

1 3-ounce can *Chinese noodles*	2 2¼-ounce cans potato sticks
1 square (1 ounce) *chocolate*	3 tablespoons cocoa plus 1 tablespoon shortening
1½ cups *corn syrup*	1 cup sugar plus ½ cup water
1 tablespoon *cornstarch*	2 tablespoons flour
1 whole *egg*	2 egg yolks plus 1 tablespoon water
1 cup sifted all-purpose *flour*	1 cup plus 2 tablespoons sifted cake flour
1½ cups diced cooked *ham*	1 12-ounce can pork luncheon meat, diced
⅔ cup *honey*	1 cup sugar plus ⅓ cup water
1 teaspoon *Italian seasoning*	¼ teaspoon each oregano, basil, thyme, and rosemary with dash of cayenne
½ pound fresh *mushrooms*	1 4-ounce can mushroom caps
1 teaspoon *oregano*	1 teaspoon marjoram
½ pound ground *pork*	½ pound sausage meat
1 teaspoon *pumpkin pie spice*	½ teaspoon cinnamon, ¼ teaspoon ginger, ⅛ teaspoon each ground nutmeg and cloves
½ cup seedless *raisins*	½ cup cut dried prunes
few drops *Tabasco*	dash of cayenne or red pepper
½ cup *tartar sauce*	6 tablespoons mayonnaise plus 2 tablespoons chopped pickle relish
1 cup *tomato juice*	½ cup tomato sauce plus ½ cup water
1 cup canned *tomatoes*	1⅓ cups chopped fresh tomatoes simmered for 10 minutes
1 teaspoon *Worcestershire sauce* ..	1 teaspoon bottled steak sauce

TABLE OF EQUIVALENTS

Bread and Crackers

1 slice bread	= ½ cup finely crumbled
18 small crackers	= 1 cup coarsely crushed
21 small crackers	= 1 cup finely crushed
9 graham cracker squares	= 1 cup coarsely crumbled
12 graham cracker squares	= 1 cup finely crumbled

1 cup potato chips, firmly
  packed   = ½ cup potato chip crumbs
12 thin pretzels   = ½ cup pretzel crumbs
26 vanilla wafers   = 1 cup finely crumbled
 9 zweiback   = 1 cup finely crumbled

Cereals and Pasta

3 cups corn flakes   = 1 cup crushed
1 cup corn meal   = 4 cups cooked
1 cup macaroni   = 2 cups cooked
1 cup noodles   = 2 cups cooked
1 cup quick-cooking oats = 1¾ cups cooked
1 cup rice   = 3 cups cooked
1 cup spaghetti   = 2 cups cooked

Dairy Products

1 cup heavy cream   = 2 cups whipped
1 pound Cheddar cheese = 4 cups shredded

Fruits

Dried:

1 pound apricots   = 3½ cups = 4½ cups cooked
1 pound figs   = 2¼ cups = 4½ cups cooked
1 pound peaches   = 3⅔ cups = 4½ cups cooked
1 pound pears   = 2⅔ cups = 5⅓ cups cooked
1 pound prunes   = 2¾ cups = 4 cups cooked
1 pound raisins   = 3¼ cups = 4 cups plumped
1 pound unpitted dates = 2½ cups = 1¾ cups pitted

Fresh:

1 pound apples   = 3 medium   = 3 cups pared, diced
1 pound cranberries = 4¾ cups   = 3¼ cups sauce
1 average lemon   = ⅛ cup pulp = 3 to 4 tablespoons juice
1 average orange   = ¼ cup pulp = ½ cup juice
1 quart red cherries   = 2 cups pitted
1 pound Tokay grapes   = 2¾ cups seeded

Nuts

1 pound soft shell almonds = 2 cups shelled
1 pound hard shell almonds = 1 cup shelled
1 pound walnuts in shell   = 2½ cups shelled
¼ pound walnut meats   = 1 cup chopped nut meats

Vegetables
Dried:

1 cup Lima beans	= 2⅓ cups cooked	
1 cup red beans	= 2 cups cooked	
1 cup white beans	= 3 cups cooked	

Fresh:

1 pound beets	= 4 medium	= 2 cups diced
1 pound cabbage		= 4 cups shredded
1 pound carrots	= 8 medium	= 4 cups diced
1 pound celery	= 2 small bunches	= 4 cups diced
12 ears corn		= 3 cups cut kernels
1 pound peas in pod		= 1 cup shelled
1 pound potatoes	= 4 medium	= 2½ cups diced